LEED O&M
MOCK EXAM

Questions, Answers, and Explanations

A Must-Have for the
LEED AP O+M Exam,
Green Building LEED Certification,
and Sustainability

Gang Chen

ArchiteG®, Inc.
Irvine, California

LEED O&M MOCK EXAM:
Questions, Answers, and Explanations: A Must-Have for the LEED AP O+M
Exam, Green Building LEED Certification, and Sustainability

Copyright © 2010 Gang Chen
Second Printing of the First Edition
Cover Design and Photo © 2010 Gang Chen

Copy Editor: Alanna Boutin

All Rights Reserved.
No part of this book may be transmitted or reproduced by any means or in any form, including electronic, graphic, or mechanical, without the express written consent of the publisher or author, except in the case of brief quotations in a review.

ArchiteG®, Inc.
http://www.ArchiteG.com

ISBN: 978-0-9843741-1-3

PRINTED IN THE UNITED STATES OF AMERICA

R0433251210

Leadership in Energy and Environmental Design
(LEED)

LEED-CERTIFIED   LEED-SILVER
LEED-GOLD   LEED-PLATINUM

LEED GREEN ASSOCIATE

LEED AP BD+C   LEED AP ID+C
LEED AP O+M
LEED AP HOMES   LEED AP ND

LEED FELLOW

Dedication

To my parents, Zhuixian and Yugen,
my wife, Xiaojie, and my daughters,
Alice, Angela, Amy, and Athena.

Disclaimer

LEED O&M Mock Exam provides general information about the LEED AP Operation and Maintenance Exam (LEED AP O+M or LEED AP O&M Exam) and LEED green building certification. For simplicity, we shall refer to this exam as LEED O&M Exam, or LEED AP O+M Exam throughout the entire book. The book is sold with the understanding that neither the publisher nor the author is providing legal, accounting, or other professional services. If legal, accounting, or other professional services are required, seek the assistance of a competent professional firm.

The purpose of this publication is not to reprint the content of all other available texts on the subject. You are urged to read other materials, and tailor them to fit your needs.

Great effort has been taken to make this resource as complete and accurate as possible; however, nobody is perfect, and there may be several typographical errors or other mistakes present. You should use this book as a general guide and not as the ultimate source on this subject. If you find any potential errors, please send an e-mail to: plantingdesign@yahoo.com

LEED O&M Mock Exam is intended to provide general, entertaining, informative, educational, and enlightening content. Neither the publisher nor the author shall be liable to anyone or any entity for any loss or damages, or alleged loss and damages, caused directly or indirectly by the content of this book.

USGBC and LEED are trademarks of the U.S. Green Building Council. The U.S. Green Building Council is not affiliated with this publication.

Contents

Preface

Chapter One: LEED O&M Mock Exam Part I: Questions, Answers, and Explanations   19

  I. Important Note: Read this before you work on LEED O&M Mock Exam
 II. LEED O&M Mock Exam Part I
III. Answers and Explanations for the LEED O&M Mock Exam Part I

Chapter Two: LEED O&M Mock Exam Part II: Questions, Answers, and Explanations   75

  I. LEED O&M Mock Exam Part II
 II. Answers and Explanations for the LEED O&M Mock Exam Part II
III. How was the LEED O&M Mock Exam created?
 IV. Latest trend for LEED Exams
  V. Where can I find the latest official sample questions for the LEED O&M Exam?
 VI. LEED O&M Exam registration

Chapter Three: Frequently Asked Questions (FAQ) and Other Useful Resources   127

1. I found the reference guide way too tedious. Can I read only your books and just refer to the USGBC reference guide (if one is available for the exam I am taking) when needed?
2. Is one week really enough time for me to prepare for the exam while I am working?
3. Would you say that if I buy books from your LEED Exam Guide series, I could pass the exam without any other study materials? The books sold on the USGBC Web site cost hundreds of dollars, so I would be quite happy if I could buy your books and only use them.
4. I am preparing for the LEED exam. Do I need to read the 2-inch thick reference guide?
5. For LEED v3.0, will the total number of points be more than 110 if a project receives all of the standard and extra credits?
6. For the exam, do I need to know the project phase in which a specific prerequisite/credit takes place? That is, pre-design, schematic design, etc.
7. Are you writing any other books for the new LEED exams? If so, what are they?
8. Important documents that you need to

download for <u>free</u>, become familiar with, and <u>memorize</u>
9. Important documents that you need to download for <u>free</u>, and become <u>familiar</u> with
10. Do I need to take many practice questions to prepare for a LEED exam?

Appendixes 139
1. Default occupancy factors
2. Important resources and further study materials you can download for <u>free</u>
3. Annotated bibliography
4. Valuable Web sites and links

Back Page Promotion 145
1. *Architectural Practice Simplified*
2. *Planting Design Illustrated*
3. LEED Exam Guide series

Index 169

Preface

There are two main purposes for *LEED O&M Mock Exam*: to help you pass the LEED O&M Exam and to assist you in understanding the process of getting building LEED certified.

The LEED O&M Exam has two parts:

Part I is EXACTLY the same as the LEED Green Associate Exam. It has 100 multiple choice questions and must be finished within 2 hours. (The total exam time for BOTH parts of the exam is 4 hours.) In this book, "LEED O&M Exam Part I," "LEED O&M Exam Part I," and "LEED Green Associate Exam" are used interchangeably since they are EXACTLY the same.

Part II is the LEED O&M specialty exam. It focuses on information and knowledge related directly to green building operation and maintenance (O&M). It also contains 100 multiple choice questions and must be finished within 2 hours.

Both parts of the LEED O&M Exam must be taken back-to-back in the same sitting. The only exception is when a test taker fails one of the two parts, he can retake only the failed part of the exam at a later date.

The raw exam score is converted to a scaled score ranging from 125 to 200. The passing score is 170 or higher. You need to answer approximately 60 questions correctly in each part to pass. There is an optional 10-minute tutorial for computer testing before the exam and an optional 10-minute exit survey.

The LEED Green Associate Exam is the most important LEED exam for two reasons:

1. You have to pass this exam in order to get the title of LEED Green Associate.

2. This exam is also the required Part I (2 hours) of ALL LEED AP+ exams. You have to pass the LEED Green Associate Exam, plus Part II (2 hours) of the specific LEED AP+ exam of your choice to get any LEED AP+ title, unless you have passed the old LEED AP Exam before June 30, 2009.

There are several ways to prepare for the LEED O&M Exam:

1. You can take USGBC courses or workshops. You should take USGBC classes at both the 100 (Awareness) and 200 (LEED Core Concepts and Strategies) level to successfully prepare for Part I of the exam. USGBC classes at the 300 level (Green Building Operation and Maintenance: The LEED Implementation Process) can be tak-

en to prepare for Part II of the exam. A 1-day course normally costs $445 (as of publication) with an early registration discount; otherwise, it is $495. The USGBC workshops or courses are offered at set times in different locations.

OR
2. Take USGBC online courses. Information is available at USGBC or GBCI Web sites. The USGBC online courses are less personal but still expensive.

OR
3. Read related books. Unfortunately, there are NO official GBCI books on the LEED O&M Exam, but some third-party books on the exam are available. *LEED O&M Mock Exam* is one of the first books to cover this subject and is available for purchase.

To stay at the forefront of LEED and the green building movement and to make my books more valuable to their readers, I signed up and completed USGBC courses and workshops. I also reviewed the USGBC and GBCI Web sites, and many other sources to acquire as much information as possible on LEED. *LEED O&M Mock Exam* is the result of my extensive research. This book is an invaluable tool for preparing for the exam.

Strategy 101 for the LEED O&M Exam is that you must recognize that you have only a limited amount of time to prepare for it. So, concentrate on the most important information contained within the book.

LEED O&M Mock Exam provides you with a complete set of mock exams, including questions, answers, and explanations.

Many people in the field have some knowledge of LEED. If you are unfamiliar with some of the book's content, I suggest you should use a highlighter to mark that information. It will help you focus on the unfamiliar material later when you review it. You can repeat this process with different colored highlighters on subsequent reads until you are very familiar with the content of this book. Preparing in this manner will prepare you to take the LEED O&M Exam.

The key to passing the LEED O&M Exam, or any other exam, is to understand the scope of the exam, and not read too many books. Select one or two really good books and focus on them. Take time to <u>understand</u> and <u>memorize</u> the content.

There is a part of the LEED O&M Exam that you can score highly on by reading study materials. You should try to answer all questions related to this part correctly.

The exam may contain questions that you may not be prepared for. For example, if you have not done actual LEED building certification, some questions may require guesswork. This could be the hardest part of the exam, but these questions should be only a small percentage of the overall test. If you are well prepared, it should not be too problematic. Remember to always <u>eliminate</u> the obviously wrong answers, and then attempt to make an educated <u>guess</u>. There is no penalty for guessing. If you have no idea what the correct answer is and cannot eliminate any obviously wrong answers, then just pick an answer and do not waste valuable time on the question. The key is to use the <u>same</u> guess answer for all of the questions that you do not know. For example, if you choose "d" as your guess answer, then you should be consistent and use "d" as your guess answer for all the other questions that you don't know. This way, you will likely have a better chance at guessing more correct answers.

This is not an easy exam, but you should be able to pass if you prepare well. If you <u>set your goal for a high score and study hard</u>, you will have a better chance of passing. If you set your goal for the minimum passing score of 170, you will probably end up scoring 169, fail, and have to <u>retake</u> the exam again. Failing is the last thing you want. Give yourself plenty of time and do not wait until the last minute to begin preparing for the exam. I have met people who have spent 40 hours preparing and passed the exam, but I suggest that you give yourself <u>at least 2 to 3 weeks</u> of preparation time. On the night before the exam, you should look through the mock exam questions you answered incorrectly and review the correct answers. Read this book carefully, prepare well, relax, and be fit physically, mentally, and psychologically on the day of the exam. Follow this advice and you will pass the exam.

Chapter One
LEED O&M Mock Exam Part I: Questions, Answers, and Explanations

Use the questions from the mock exam to prepare for the real exam. They will give you an idea of what the GBCI is looking for on the LEED O&M Exam, and how the questions will be asked. If you can answer 60% of the sample questions correctly, you are ready to take the real exam. The 60% passing score is based on feedback from previous readers. You should read the study materials available at least three times before you attempt the mock exam. Similar to the real exam, a question might ask you to pick one, two, or three correct answers out of four, or four correct answers out of five (some LEED exam questions have five choices). Generally speaking, if you do not know any of the correct answers, then you will probably get the overall answer wrong. You need to know the LEED system very well in order to answer correctly.

I have intentionally included some questions that you may not know the answers to. This is to help you practice making an educated guess.

I. Important Note: Read this before you work on LEED O&M Mock Exam

1. How much time should you spend on preparing for the LEED exam?

Answer: Some people spend too much time preparing for the LEED exam, and by the time they take the real test, they may have forgotten a lot of the information already.

Timing is VERY critical. If you pass the practice test with a score of 190 three months before the real test, by the time you take the test, you may have forgotten the information and score much lower.

One way to overcome this is NOT to take too much time to prepare for the LEED exam, and save at least one set of mock exam to use in the last week before the exam. You should NOT read any questions on this reserved mock exam until one or two weeks before the exam. This way, you can alert and energize yourself one more time right before the real exam, and work on your weaknesses. You can save the LEED O&M Mock Exam for this purpose.

There is one reader who passed the LEED Green Associate Exam or Part I of LEED AP O&M Exam by studying my other book, *LEED GA Exam Guide,* for 3 days.

For an average reader, I recommend not less than 2 weeks, but not MORE than 2 months of prep time. If you read my other book, *LEED GA Exam Guide*, you'll understand why too much prep time may hurt your chance of passing the exam.

II. LEED O&M Mock Exam Part I

1. With regard to the credit, Optimize Energy Performance, who has the most influence in decision-making?
   a. MEP Engineer
   b. Architect
   c. Contractor
   d. Health Department Plan Checker

2. A project team should include the following as part of process energy: (Choose 3)
   a. Lighting that is part of the medical equipment
   b. Lighting included as part of the lighting power allowance
   c. Energy for water pumps
   d. HVAC
   e. Energy for elevators and escalators

3. A project team should include the following as part of regulated (non-process) energy: (Choose 3)
   a. Lighting for interiors
   b. Refrigeration and kitchen cooking

c. Space heating
d. Service water heating
e. Energy for computers, office, and general miscellaneous equipment

4. With regard to LEED v3.0, which of the following LEED rating systems has the most points for the WE category?
   a. LEED NC
   b. LEED CS
   c. LEED Schools
   d. LEED CI
   e. LEED O&M

5. Which of the following are not considered laws?
   a. USGBC LEED reference guides
   b. Building codes
   c. ADA
   d. Municipal codes
   e. EPA Codes of Federal Regulations

6. Which of the following buildings cannot obtain LEED certification? (Choose 2)
   a. A new building that uses CFC
   b. A new building that does not use CFC
   c. A remodel project with a plan to phase out CFCs in 15 years
   d. A building that uses natural refrigerants
   e. A building that uses dry ice

7. Which of the following can reduce stormwater runoff and alleviate the urban heat island

effect? (Choose 3)
a. Increasing the site coverage ratio
b. Increasing Floor Area Ratio (FAR)
c. Using a vegetated roof
d. Using porous pavement with high albedo
e. Building a retention pond on the site

8. Recycled materials will contribute to which of the following?
a. Traffic alleviation and smog reduction
b. Protection of virgin materials
c. Energy savings
d. MEP cost savings

9. Which of the following is not graywater?
a. Water from kitchen sinks
b. Water from toilet
c. Harvest rainwater
d. Water from outdoor area drains
e. None of above
f. All of above

10. Which of the following is not blackwater? (Choose 2)
a. Water from kitchen sinks
b. Water from toilets
c. Harvest rainwater
d. Water from floor drains
e. Rainwater that has come into contact with animal waste

11. Which of the following is not true? (Choose 2)

a. Water from kitchen sinks can be reused for landscape irrigation or flushing toilets.
b. Water from kitchen sinks cannot be reused for landscape irrigation or flushing toilets.
c. Reclaimed water requires special piping with a different color.
d. Reclaimed water cannot reduce potable water use.

12. Which of the following sets the baseline for water use? (Choose 2)
    a. Energy Policy Act (EPAct) of 1992
    b. Uniform Plumbing Code (UPC)
    c. WaterSense standards
    d. International Plumbing Code (IPC)

13. Which of the following sets the minimum standard of water use reduction?
    a. Energy Policy Act (EPAct) of 1992
    b. Uniform Plumbing Codes (UPC)
    c. WaterSense standards
    d. International Plumbing Code (IPC)

14. The State of California is building a visitor center on a 200,000 sf park. How big does the visitor center need to be, in order to meet the MPRs for LEED?
    a. 1,000 sf
    b. 2,000 sf
    c. 3,000 sf
    d. 4,000 sf

e. There is not enough information to determine the minimum sf of the visitor center.

15. What is the maximum number of Regional Priority points a project can achieve?
   a. 3
   b. 4
   c. 5
   d. 6

16. The LEED O&M rating system is different from other LEED rating systems in which of the following ways:
   a. The LEED O&M rating system can be applied to any building type.
   b. The LEED O&M rating system emphasizes measuring and verification.
   c. The LEED O&M rating system emphasizes life cycle costing.
   d. The LEED O&M rating system deals with buildings after construction is completed.

17. Which program is used to qualify off-site green power for LEED?
   a. Green-e
   b. Center for Resource Solution
   c. Green Label
   d. Green Certified

18. Which of the following is the best to measure a material's ability to reflect sunshine?

a. Albedo
b. SRI
c. Color
d. Hue

19. Which of the following will not reduce materials sent to landfill? (Choose 2)
    a. Recycling
    b. Reusing materials
    c. Using reground materials
    d. Reducing materials used
    e. Reworking

20. Which of the following will not reduce materials sent to recycling facilities?
    a. Recycling
    b. Reusing materials
    c. Reducing materials used
    d. Reworking

21. Which of the following is the best statement regarding water savings for LEED credits?
    a. Water savings for LEED credits are per building codes.
    b. Water savings for LEED credits are per green building codes.
    c. Water savings for LEED credits are per federal regulations.
    d. Water savings for LEED credits are based on the percentage of water savings achieved by each design case as compared with a baseline building.

22. Which of the following is the best way to alleviate suburban sprawl?
    a. Build more low-rise, high-density housing.
    b. Provide underground parking spaces.
    c. Improve community connectivity.
    d. Provide more pedestrian walkways.

23. A developer has selected an urban site near a shopping center. This will help which of the following?
    a. Community connectivity
    b. Reducing urban runoff
    c. Community relationship
    d. Minimum city code requirements

24. Which of the following are considered open spaces for a LEED project?
    a. Landscape areas
    b. Tennis courts
    c. Sidewalks
    d. Areas under canopy
    e. Atriums with views to the ocean

25. A project seeking LEED certification may incur extra time for the following except:
    a. team member meetings.
    b. a city's plan check.
    c. commissioning.
    d. construction administration.

26. When should a project team start to plan a building's LEED certification?

a. At schematic design
b. At design development
c. At pre-design stage
d. At construction stage

27. For LEED certification, you should include the following as part of the project's area except:
    a. a parking lot.
    b. a landscape area.
    c. an interior space.
    d. a shared parking structure on an adjacent property.

28. A project team is working on a LEED NC project. How much CFC-refrigerant can the team use?
    a. 2%
    b. 5%
    c. 7%
    d. None

29. Green-e is used for which of the following?
    a. On-site green energy
    b. On-site renewable energy
    c. Off-site renewable energy
    d. None of the above

30. Zero Emission Vehicles (ZEV) are defined by the standards set up by: (Choose 2)
    a. California Air Resources Board
    b. Center for Resource Solution
    c. ACEEE

d. SCAQMD

31. You are working on a remodel project seeking LEED certification. What should you do about the existing HVAC units containing CFCs?
    a. Replace CFCs with dry ice.
    b. Replace CFCs with natural refrigerant.
    c. Replace CFCs with halons.
    d. Phase out CFCs in 10 years.

32. Which of the following is graywater?
    a. Water from bathroom sinks and kitchen sinks
    b. Water from bathtubs
    c. Water from toilets
    d. Rainwater collected in cisterns
    e. Stormwater that has not come in contract with toilet waste

33. For a building using a halon-based fire suppression system, which of the following is true? (Choose 2)
    a. Halons cause damage to the ozone layer.
    b. This building cannot seek LEED certification.
    c. This building must meet Fire Department requirements concerning halons.
    d. The halons must have a leakage rate of 10% or less.

34. What is the fundamental reason for global warming?

a. Too many cars on the street
b. The use of biofuel
c. Too many green houses were built in the past century
d. Too much carbon dioxide
e. Ozone depletion

35. SMACNA address which of the following items related to LEED?
    a. Metal work
    b. VOCs
    c. Air quality during construction
    d. ODP
    e. Certified wood

36. For a project's initial research, what are some of the most important local issues? (Choose 3)
    a. Site orientation
    b. Parking regulations
    c. Incentives for sustainable design
    d. ACEEE
    e. TRCs

37. Which of the following statements are not true? (Choose 2)
    a. Bicycle racks will help community connectivity.
    b. High SRI pavement will alleviate the heat island effect.
    c. Green roofs can reduce stormwater runoff and alleviate the heat island effect.
    d. Retention ponds will not reduce storm-

water runoff.

38. A construction waste management plan should include which of the following?
    a. The recycling capacity of the neighborhood recycle center
    b. The location and size of the recycle areas
    c. If the existing ceiling should be reused
    d. The percentage of reused materials

39. A project team is seeking LEED certification for a building. The project can be certified under either the LEED NC or LEED CS rating system. How should the project team determine which LEED system to use? (Choose 2)
    a. Use the system that can gain most points for LEED.
    b. Ask the landlord for advice.
    c. Use the 40/60 rule.
    d. Make an independent decision.
    e. Use the 30/70 rule.

40. A project team is seeking LEED NC certification for a building. Which of the following is true?
    a. The project team cannot seek precertification as a marketing tool for funding and attracting tenants.
    b. The project team can seek precertification as a marketing tool for funding and attracting tenants.

c. The project must have a signed lease or LOI for at least 70% of the spaces.
d. The project must be located in a new neighborhood.

41. A project team created a drive-by recycling program for the general public to recycle batteries and used electronics. The project team can gain a point under which of the following categories?
    a. SS
    b. MR
    c. ID
    d. IEQ

42. What kinds of energy will generate the most pollution? (Choose 3)
    a. Wind
    b. Biofuel
    c. Gas
    d. Natural gas
    e. Nuclear power

43. Which of the following water saving items can be used for outdoor, indoor, and processed water? (Choose 2)
    a. Water efficient fixtures
    b. Sub-meters
    c. Native plants
    d. Water saving education programs

44. Which of the following analyze the potential savings over a building's life span?

a. ROI
   b. Life-cycle analysis
   c. Life-cycle cost analysis
   d. Life-cycle saving analysis

45. Which of the following includes standards regarding major factors affecting human comfort?
   a. ASHRAE 55-2004
   b. ASHRAE 62.1-2007
   c. Green Label Plus
   d. Green Building Index

46. If you pass the LEED Green Associate Exam, what can you use on your business card?
   a. The GBCI logo
   b. The LEED GA logo per USGBC guidelines
   c. The LEED GA logo per GBCI guidelines
   d. The LEED Green Associate logo per GBCI guidelines
   e. The LEED GA designation only without any logo

47. A tenant purchased some furniture containing VOCs that was manufactured 450 miles from the job site. Which of the following LEED categories will be affected?
   a. SS
   b. EA
   c. MR

d. IEQ
e. This project cannot seek LEED certification.

48. Green building through a holistic design approach will result in which of the following?
   a. Longer construction time
   b. Shorter construction time
   c. Extra cost
   d. Synergy
   e. Savings over a building's lifetime

49. A project team is seeking LEED certification for an 8-story building. The building has 8 equal floors, and the total square footage of the building is 168,000 sf. What is the building's footprint?
   a. 168,000 sf
   b. 42,000 sf
   c. 21,000 sf
   d. None of the above

50. For the same project mentioned in Question 49, if the total site area is 1 acre, what is the site coverage for this project?
   a. 48%
   b. 46%
   c. 43%
   d. 38%

51. For the same project mentioned in Question 49, if the total buildable site area is 1 acre, what is the FAR for this project?

a. 438%
b. 386%
c. 338%
d. 298%

52. A project team is working on a LEED project composed of 6 buildings on a campus. Each building is located on a 1 acre parcel of land. How should the project team determine the boundary of the LEED project?
    a. Each building should have its own LEED project boundary at the edge of the 1 acre land.
    b. The LEED project boundary should be the perimeter of the 6 acre site.
    c. The project team can make its own decision and determine the LEED project boundary.
    d. There is not enough information to determine the LEED project boundary.

53. A LEED project's landscape area includes which of the following?
    a. Green roofs
    b. Naturalistically designed retention ponds
    c. Sidewalks
    d. Vegetated roofs

54. Which of the following applies to the LEED EA category? (Choose 2)
    a. ASHRAE Advanced Energy Design Guide for Retail Buildings 2006

b. ASHRAE Standard 55-2004
c. ASHRAE 62.1-2007
d. ASHRAE/IESNA Standard 90.1-2007

55. Which of the following is considered a project soft cost?
    a. Carpet
    b. Doors
    c. Permit Fees
    d. Trees and shrubs

56. Where can a LEED Green Associate find the latest errata for LEED reference guides on-line?
    a. www.gbci.org
    b. www.nrdc.org
    c. www.usgbc.org
    d. www.epa.gov

57. The heat island effect can typically create ___ degrees Fahrenheit of change in temperature?
    a. 1
    b. 5
    c. 10
    d. 20

58. Who rules on CIRs?
    a. The Technical Advisory Group
    b. The LEED Administrator
    c. GBCI
    d. USGBC

59. Which of the following standards specifies minimum ventilation rates for IAQ Performance?
   a. ASHRAE 52.2-1999
   b. ASHRAE 62.1-2007
   c. ASHRAE/IESNA Standard 90.1-2007
   d. ASTM

60. Who of the following publishes GWP and ODP scores?
   a. The World Meteorological Organization
   b. ASTM
   c. USGBC
   d. The Global Climate Control Board

61. Which of the following are the most commonly used energy codes in the United States?
   a. Universal Energy Conservation Codes
   b. IPC by International Code Council
   c. International Energy Conservation Codes
   d. Energy Rating Codes

62. Which of the following is the most effective way to reduce stormwater runoff?
   a. Building a roof with high SRI value
   b. Using pavers with high albedo
   c. Grouping buildings together
   d. Adding trees to a parking lot

63. Which of the following sites is the best for community connectivity?

- a. A site close to the ocean
- b. A site close to a train station
- c. A brownfield site
- d. A site close to a shopping center

64. Choose the non-alternative-fuel vehicle from the following.
    - a. A hybrid car
    - b. A bus powered by natural gas with at least 20 mpg
    - c. A fuel-efficient car powered by gas with at least 40 mpg
    - d. An electric car

65. Which of the following is a car share membership program?
    - a. Three or more people going to work in the same vehicle
    - b. A program in which two or more people share the cost of a parking space
    - c. A shuttle service program from a train station to work places
    - d. A program for people to rent a vehicle on a daily or hourly basis

66. Which of the following must be certified under only one LEED rating system?
    - a. 100% of the LEED project gross floor area
    - b. 80% of the LEED project gross floor area
    - c. Everything inside the property boundary
    - d. 100% of the LEED project gross site

area

67. Which of the following is graywater?
    a. Stormwater
    b. Laundry water
    c. Dishwasher water
    d. Water in retention ponds

68. Which of the following is used to measure a LEED building's environmental performance?
    a. Life cycle analysis
    b. Cradle-to-cradle analysis
    c. Whole building perspective
    d. Integrated design approach
    e. Overall energy reduction

69. If a LEED project has a CFC phase-out plan, which of the following must occur?
    a. The project can only allow 5% or less of annual CFC leakage.
    b. CFC must be replaced within 15 years.
    c. CFC must be replaced with CO_2.
    d. CFC must be replaced with halons.

70. Which two of the following have the same meaning?
    a. Albedo
    b. SRI
    c. Refraction
    d. Reflection
    e. Solar Reflectance

71. What are RECs?
    a. The amount of fossil fuels avoided by buying renewable energy and expressed in kilograms
    b. The positive attributes of power generated by renewable sources
    c. The amount of renewable energy purchased from a third party approved by the Green-e program
    d. None of the above

72. The priorities for LEED projects are based on: (Choose 2)
    a. Costs and benefits
    b. Environmental guidelines
    c. Carbon footprint
    d. Project constraints

73. Construction waste reduction strategies include which of the following?
    a. Purchasing materials manufactured locally
    b. Using durable materials
    c. Donating unused materials to charities
    d. Burning the construction waste on site

74. Which of the following is the foundation of the LEED building rating system?
    a. Prerequisites
    b. MPRs
    c. Prerequisites and credits
    d. The triple bottom line

75. A project team is seeking LEED NC certification for a 3-story residential building. Each floor is 600 sf. Which of the following is true?
   a. The project team can seek LEED NC certification because the building is less than 100,000 sf.
   b. The project team can seek LEED NC certification because the building is more than 1,000 sf.
   c. The project team cannot seek LEED NC certification.
   d. The project team can seek LEED NC certification because it meets LEED's MPRs.

76. Per Montreal Protocol, HCFCs have to be phased out by:
   a. 1995
   b. 2010
   c. 2011
   d. 2030

77. If a building's wastewater overflows, which of the following can come into contact with potable water? (Choose 2)
   a. CO
   b. Toxic metal
   c. Grease
   d. Halons

78. The best way to prevent environmental impact caused by refrigerant leakage is to:

a. Choose high quality plumbing materials, and perform high quality installation and maintenance.
b. Use refrigerants without ODP.
c. Design a building with natural ventilation and use no refrigerants.
d. None of the above

79. A project team is seeking LEED certification for a single building. What does the LEED project boundary include? (Choose 2)
a. Only the portion of the site submitted by the project team for LEED certification
b. Overlaps with the edge of the building
c. Overlaps with the edge of the development
d. The entire project scope of work

80. The economic benefits of green buildings include: (Choose 2)
a. Reduced disturbance of wetland
b. Lower water bills
c. Increased use of rapidly renewable materials
d. Better IEQ and less liabilities

81. Which of the following is not a fossil fuel? (Choose 2)
a. Gas
b. Natural gas
c. Biofuel
d. Solar power

82. Which of the following needs to be implemented for water efficiency?
    a. A baseline of water use
    b. HET
    c. Waterless urinals
    d. Xeriscape

83. Which of the following is the most important feature of durability?
    a. The ability to endure and last for a long time
    b. Low maintenance
    c. Little or no unexpected extra costs
    d. Low maintenance and operation expense over the lifetime of the product

84. A project team is preparing a construction waste management plan. Which of the following should be included? (Choose 2)
    a. The removal of refrigerants containing ODP and GWP
    b. Recycle areas
    c. The removal and disposal of hazardous materials like PCBs
    d. The reduction of building size

85. For a LEED project, which of the following should not be used in a fire suppression system? (Choose 2)
    a. Dry ice
    b. Water
    c. HCFCs
    d. CFCs

86. Which of the following can earn points for Innovation in Design?
    a. Meeting the requirements of all LEED prerequisites and credits
    b. Exceptional performance above and beyond the LEED requirements for an existing credit
    c. Finding a solution responding to the project's regional priorities
    d. Innovative performance in green building categories not covered by an existing LEED credit

87. A project team uses a strategy to earn an ID point for a project in California. Which of the following is true?
    a. The same strategy can be used and guaranteed for an ID point in other projects.
    b. The same strategy can be used for other projects in the same region.
    c. The same strategy may or may not earn an ID point in another project.
    d. None of the above

88. An office building uses ammonia (NH3) as a refrigerant. Which of the following is true?
    a. NH3 has a higher ODP than HCFC.
    b. NH3 has a lower GWP than HCFC.
    c. NH3 is easier to leak out than HCFC.
    d. CFC is easier to leak out than HCFC.

89. A project team is seeking extra points under the Innovation in Design credit category.

Which of the following is a feasible strategy?
a. Set up a display area inside the building to educate the public on this building's LEED performance.
b. Try to gain more points than the original target level of LEED certification.
c. Double the performance for a LEED credit.
d. None of the above

90. Which of the following can be the most efficient way to save energy?
a. Proper building orientation and fenestration
b. High performance HVAC systems
c. LEED certified equipment
d. None of the above

91. Which of the following is not true?
a. A LEED project team has to review the USGBC or GBCI website for previously submitted CIRs before submitting a new one.
b. A LEED project team has to review the USGBC reference guide before submitting a CIR.
c. All LEED rating systems can have CIRs except LEED ND.
d. A fee has to be paid for each CIR submitted.

92. ASHRAE standards apply to all of the following except:
    a. SS
    b. WE
    c. IEQ
    d. EA

93. Rainwater is:
    a. potable water.
    b. non-potable water.
    c. blackwater.
    d. raw water.
    e. graywater.

94. What are the most important criteria for a LEED building rating system?
    a. Quantifiable performances
    b. Prerequisites
    c. Credits
    d. Third party evaluations
    e. Third party standards

95. Which of the following cannot save water for landscape irrigation? (Choose 2)
    a. Mulches
    b. Perennials
    c. Hardscape
    d. Overhead irrigation
    e. Head to head coverage

96. Energy used by elevators and escalators is:
    a. process energy.
    b. non-process energy.

c. regulated energy.
d. renewable energy.
e. non-renewable energy.

97. Which of the following are most appropriate for a vegetated roof?
    a. Native plants
    b. Trees with large canopies
    c. Adaptive plants
    d. Lightweight plants
    e. There is not enough information to answer this question.

98. Which of the following is a prerequisite for purchasing green power? (Choose 3)
    a. The completion of the commissioning plan
    b. Communication with the key stakeholders
    c. Consultation with an electrical engineer
    d. Compilation of energy data
    e. Evaluation of onsite and offsite energy choices

99. Which of the following is a pre-consumer recycled item?
    a. Aluminum storefront created from materials reclaimed from the manufacturing process
    b. Demolition concrete pieces used at another project
    c. Rigid insulation created from materials reclaimed from the manufacturing

process of form cornice
   d. Scraps re-used in the carpet manufacturing process

100. A project team is seeking LEED Platinum certification for a school project. When can the project team advise the school board that the LEED Platinum certification has been achieved?
   a. After the project's substantial completion
   b. After the LEED registration is approved
   c. After the design review
   d. After the construction review
   e. After the LEED application is reviewed and approved by GBCI

III. Answers and Explanations for the LEED O&M Mock Exam Part I

1. Answer: a
   The MEP Engineer has the most influence in energy performance, and the credit, Optimize Energy Performance.

2. Answer: a, c, and e
   The project team should include the following as part of **process energy**:
   Refrigeration and kitchen cooking, laundry (washing and drying), elevators and escalators, computers, office and general miscellaneous equipment, lighting not included in

the lighting power allowance (such as lighting that is part of the medical equipment), and other uses like water pumps, etc.

3. Answer: a, c, and d
   The project team should include the following as **regulated (non-process) energy**: HVAC, exhaust fans and hoods, lighting for interiors, surface parking, garage parking, building façade and grounds, space heating, and service water heating, etc.

4. Answer: e
   Points for the WE category:
   a. LEED NC: 10 points
   b. LEED CS: 10 points
   c. LEED Schools: 11 points
   d. LEED CI: 11 points
   e. LEED O&M: 14 points

5. Answer: a
   Buildings codes, ADA, Municipal codes, and EPA Codes of Federal Regulations are laws, because they have gone through the legislation process, but reference guides by USGBC are NOT laws. They are rules set by the USGBC and have NO legal authority like the other governing agencies.

   LEED standards are voluntary. You choose to obey the rules when you seek certification for a building, but these rules are NOT laws.

6. Answer: a and c
   The manufacture of HVAC units containing CFCs was stopped in the United States in 1995. These units will be phased out from existing buildings located in the United States by 2011.

7. Answer: c, d, and e
   Increasing the site coverage or FAR will increase impervious area and will increase stormwater runoff. Porous pavement will help recharge the groundwater thereby reducing stormwater runoff, and high-albedo (high-reflectivity) materials will increase reflectivity to alleviate the urban "heat island" effect. Vegetated roofs and retention ponds can also reduce stormwater runoff and alleviate the urban "heat island" effect.

8. Answer: b
   Recycled materials can protect virgin materials, but may require more energy to process, can increase traffic, and increase MEP cost.

9. Answer: f
   Graywater is the household water that has not come into contact with the kitchen sink or toilet waste.

   See USGBC Definitions at the link below:

Chapter 1 • 51

https://www.usgbc.org/ShowFile.aspx?DocumentID=5744

The definitions on the PDF file that you can download from the link above should be read at least three times. Become very familiar with them and MEMORIZE. LEED exams always test these definitions.

10. Answer: c and d
Blackwater, otherwise known as brown water, foul water, or sewage, is water from the kitchen sink, dishwasher, or water that has come into contact with human or animal waste.

11. Answer: a and d
Read the question carefully; it is asking for the WRONG statements.

12. Answer: b and d
Both the Uniform Plumbing Code (**UPC**) and International Plumbing Code (**IPC**) set standards for plumbing fixture water use, and their requirements for the water use baseline are the same in many cases.

13. Answer: a
This question tests your knowledge of the Energy Policy Act (EPAct) of 1992. Although called the Energy Policy Act, it deals with water savings. This is the trick.

14. Answer: d

MPRs include some very basic requirements. For example:
1) The building must be 1,000 sf minimum for LEED-NC, LEED Schools, LEED-CS, and LEED-EB: O&M. There is a 250 sf minimum for LEED-CI.
2) The building to site ratio must be 2% or higher. 2% x 200,000 sf = 4,000 sf

15. Answer: b
The maximum number of Regional Priority points a project can achieve is 4 out of the 6 possible points. A project team needs to select which 4 of the 6 points to use.

16. Answer: d
The LEED O&M rating system deals with buildings after construction is completed. All other answers are not unique to LEED O&M.

17. Answer: a
You should use the definition of a renewable source given by the Center for Resource Solution's (CRS) in their Green-e product requirements to determine which power to purchase. The question is asking for a program, not an organization. Center for Resource Solution's (CRS) is an organization, while Green-e is a program.

18. Answer: b
Both albedo and SRI are good indexes, but

SRI is the better option. SRI stands for Solar Reflectance Index.

19. Answer: c and e

    Pay attention to the word "not" in the question.

20. Answer: a

    When you recycle, materials are sent to recycling facilities.

21. Answer: d

    LEED is a system set up by USGBC, and not by the federal government or International Code Council (ICC). USGBC is NOT a government agency. Building codes and green building codes are set up by the local government per the ICC model codes.

    For LEED, water savings are based on the percentage of water saved by the design case when compared with a baseline building.

22. Answer: c

    Community connectivity is the best answer. The other answers have some merit, but they are not the best answer.

23. Answer: a

    Community connectivity is the best answer. All other answers are distracters to confuse you. If you have a firm knowledge of community connectivity, you should be able to answer this question correctly.

24. Answer: a

    Open spaces need to be vegetated and pervious areas. Areas under canopy and atriums with views to the ocean are typically not considered open spaces for a LEED project.

25. Answer: b

    Pay attention to the word "except" in the question. LEED certification does NOT involve extra time or effort for a city's plan check or permitting.

26. Answer: c

    For planning a project's LEED certification, the earlier this is done in the process, the better.

27. Answer: d

    You cannot include a shared parking structure on an adjacent property as part of the project area, because it belongs to someone other than your project owner.

28. Answer: d

    You cannot use CFC-refrigerant in new buildings. LEED NC is a rating system for new buildings.

29. Answer: c

    Green-e product requirements written by the Center for Resource Solutions are used as guidelines for purchasing your building's electricity from <u>off-site</u> renewable sources. The purchase is based on quantity, NOT the cost, and contracts for this renewable energy should be at least <u>two years</u> long."

30. Answer: a and c
Only vehicles classified as **Zero Emission Vehicles (ZEV)** by California Air Resources Board or vehicles with a green score of at least <u>40</u> on the **American Council for an Energy Efficient Economy (ACEEE)** annual vehicle rating guide are qualified as fuel efficient and low emitting vehicles for LEED credit.

31. Answer: b
The manufacture of HVAC units containing CFCs was stopped in the United States in 1995. These units will be phased out from existing U.S. buildings by 2011. Halons are used for fire suppression systems, NOT HVAC systems. Dry ice is commonly used to preserve food, instead of being used as HVAC refrigerant.

32. Answer: b
Per UPC, **graywater** is the household water that has not come into contact with the kitchen sink or toilet waste.

33. Answer: a and c
Halons cause damage to the ozone layer, but

a building using a halon-based fire suppression system can still seek LEED certification. This building must meet Fire Department requirements concerning halons.

34. Answer: d
Answers "a" and "b" have some merit, but they are not the fundamental cause of global warming. The rest of the answers are simply distracters.

35. Answer: c
The <u>Sheet Metal and Air Conditioning National Contractors Association (SMACNA)</u> has an IAQ Guideline for Occupied Buildings under Construction.

36. Answer: a, b, and c
American Council for an Energy Efficient Economy (ACEEE) and Tradable Renewable Certificates (TRCs) are universal and not local issues.

37. Answer: a and d
Please note that we are looking for statements that are <u>NOT</u> true. Bicycle racks will <u>NOT</u> help community connectivity. Retention ponds will reduce stormwater runoff.

38. Answer: b
A construction waste management plan should include the location and size of the recycle areas. Answers "c" and "d" should

be part of the design phase decisions. The recycling capacity of the neighborhood recycle center does NOT need to be part of the construction waste management plan.

39. Answer: c and d
Using the system that can gain the most points for LEED makes sense, but is not mandated by USGBC. Asking a landlord for advice is not a good choice and is NOT professional; the project team should be the advisor for the landlord. Using the 40/60 rule is correct. The **40/60 rule for LEED**: if a LEED system applies to 40% or less of the project or spaces, do not use it; if a LEED system applies to 60% or more of the project or spaces, use it. In the end, the project team makes an independent and final decision.

See "LEED Rating System Selection Policy" at the link below:

http://www.usgbc.org/ShowFile.aspx?DocumentID=6667

Read this free document at least three times, because it is VERY important, and explains when to use each LEED system.

40. Answer: a
The project team cannot seek precertification as a marketing tool for funding and attracting tenants, because precertification is

for the LEED CS (Core and Shell) rating system ONLY. If the project has a signed lease or LOI for at least 70% of the spaces, this is good, but NOT required by GBCI. GBCI also does NOT require the project to be located in a new neighborhood for LEED NC.

41. Answer: c

The project team can gain a point under ID because this program provides <u>quantitative</u> performance improvements for environmental benefit, which is <u>substantially</u> better than typical sustainable practice, and is applicable to <u>other</u> projects. Answer "b" is incorrect because the recycling credit for MR involves the building occupants (not the general public), and is limited to the following materials only:

<u>P</u>aper
<u>C</u>ardboard
<u>M</u>etal
<u>G</u>lass
<u>P</u>lastics

Mnemonics: People <u>C</u>an <u>M</u>ake <u>G</u>reen <u>P</u>romises

42. Answer: c, d, and e

Wind and biofuel are clean energy. Natural gas is pretty clean, but still generates air pollution.

43. Answer: b and d

    Using water efficient fixtures applies only to indoor water; using native plants applies only to outdoor water; using sub-meters can monitor water leakage, and applies to all three cases. Water saving education programs can help teach all building users to save water, and applies to all three cases as well.

44. Answer: c

    ROI is a return on investment; life-cycle analysis is used to analyze the <u>environmental</u> impact of a building over its lifetime; life-cycle cost analysis is used to analyze the cost/savings of a building over its lifetime; life-cycle saving analysis is a distracter, and this term does not exist.

45. Answer: a

    ASHRAE 55-2004 includes standards regarding major factors affecting human comfort, such as temperature, humidity, air speed, etc. ASHRAE 62.1-2007 is related to natural ventilation; the Carpet and Rug Institute's Green Label Plus program is in regards to carpet and rugs; Green Building Index is a sustainable building rating tool used in Malaysia.

46. Answer: d

    If you pass the LEED Green Associate Exam, you can use the LEED Green Associate title or logo per GBCI guidelines on your business card. This question is testing your knowledge about the different scope of work done by GBCI and USGBC, and the proper use of the LEED Green Associate title or logo. Per GBCI, LEED GA is never an approved abbreviation of the LEED Green Associate title or logo.

I use LEED GA as part of this book's main title simply because it is more legible on Amazon.com than using the full LEED Green Associate title.

47. Answer: d
Furniture containing VOCs will affect IEQ. The "450 miles from the job site" is included as a distracter.

48. Answer: d
Green building through a holistic design approach has no definite relationship to construction time, cost, or savings over a building's lifetime. The design approach does improve the synergy of LEED credits.

49. Answer: c
The building's footprint = the first floor area = 168,000 sf/8 = 21,000 sf

50. Answer: a
1 acre = 43,560 sf. The site coverage = the

first floor area/site area = 21,000/43,560 = 48%. This question tests your basic construction knowledge: 1 acre = 43,560 sf and the concept of site coverage.

51. Answer: b
FAR (Floor Area Ratio) = the total building area/total **buildable** site area = 168,000/43,560 = 386%. This question tests your basic construction knowledge: 1 acre = 43,560 sf.

This question also tests your knowledge of USGBC's definition of FAR which is TOTALLY different from what we are used to in the construction industry. I think this one will throw many people off. It's a good trick.

See USGBC Definitions at the link below:

https://www.usgbc.org/ShowFile.aspx?DocumentID=5744

52. Answer: c
For a single building project, the perimeter of the LEED project is typically the project's boundary; for a multi-building project, the LEED project team can choose a portion of the project site to submit as the LEED project boundary.

53. Answer: d
Green roofs include vegetated roofs and

light color reflective roofs. Light color reflective roofs are NOT landscape areas. Retention ponds and sidewalks are not considered landscape areas. The best answer is vegetated roofs.

54. Answer: a and d
 Answers "b" and "c" are standards for the LEED IEQ category.

55. Answer: c
 All the other answers are hard costs (material costs).

56. Answer: c
 USGBC is in charge of creating all reference guides and the related errata.

57. Answer: c
 Pay attention to the word "typically."

58. Answer: a
 Technical Advisory Group is the best answer. The LEED Administrator is a distracter. USGBC is no longer involved with building LEED certification. GBCI depends on the Technical Advisory Group for CIRs.

59. Answer: b
 See IEQp1.

60. Answer: a
 ASTM and USGBC do not publish GWP

and ODP scores. The Global Climate Control Board does not exist.

61. Answer: c

    Universal Energy Conservation Codes and Energy Rating Codes do not exist. IPC stands for International Plumbing Code.

62. Answer: c

    High SRI value and albedo can help alleviate the heat island effect. Adding trees to a parking lot can reduce stormwater runoff to some extent, but grouping buildings together can reduce the hardscape areas, and is the most effective way to reduce stormwater runoff.

63. Answer: d

    The qualified Basic Services that can help to gain LEED points for community connectivity include, but are not limited to:
    a) Place of Worship
    b) Restaurant
    c) Supermarket
    d) Convenience Grocery
    e) Laundry
    f) Cleaner
    g) Beauty Salon
    h) Hardware
    i) Pharmacy
    j) Medical/Dental
    k) Bank
    l) Senior Care Facility

m) Community Center
n) Fitness Center
o) Daycare
p) School
q) Library
r) Museum
s) Theater
t) Park
u) Fire Station
v) Post Office

A shopping center includes many of the basic services listed above, and is the best choice.

64. Answer: c
A car powered by gas is a non-alternative-fuel vehicle

65. Answer: d
Answer "a" is considered carpooling; Answer "b" is simply sharing parking cost; and Answer "c" is a shuttle service program.

66. Answer: a
A project team does NOT need to certify everything inside the property boundary, and can determine the LEED project site boundary for LEED submittal and certification.

67. Answer: b
Per UPC, **graywater** is household water that has not come into contact with kitchen sinks,

human excretion, or animal waste. Graywater includes used water from bathroom washbasins, bathtubs, showers, and water from laundry tubs and clothes washers. Graywater does not include water from dishwashers or kitchen sinks.

68. Answer: c
Cradle-to-cradle analysis is the same as life cycle analysis, eco-balance, or life cycle assessment, and is used to evaluate the environmental impact of a <u>service</u> or <u>product</u>. We use whole building perspective for LEED. Energy reduction is only one aspect of LEED. LEED includes other categories, such as SS, WE, IEQ, etc. Integrated design approach is a design approach that includes consideration for <u>people, planet and profit</u> (triple bottom line or three Ps).

69. Answer: a
CFC can be replaced with CO_2 or other refrigerants. Halons are used for fire suppression systems. The manufacture of HVAC units containing CFCs was stopped in the United States in 1995. These units will be phased out from existing buildings located in the United States by 2011.

70. Answer: a and e
SRI stands for Solar Reflectance Index. Albedo means solar reflectance.

71. Answer: b
RECs mean Renewable Energy Certificates. They represent positive attributes of power generated by renewable sources. When you purchase RECs, you are buying the attributes, NOT necessarily the real power used in your project. Anyone can purchase RECs from anywhere, even if the power used in his/her project is not green power. The money s/he pays allows others to generate or use green power, and achieves overall reduction of the use of fossil fuels in the world. This is a marketing approach for sustainability.

72. Answer: b and d
Per USGBC, the priorities for LEED projects are based on environmental guidelines and project constraints.

73. Answer: c
Burning construction waste on site is not acceptable. Answers "a" and "b" are good practice, but they cannot reduce <u>construction</u> waste.

74. Answer: d
Prerequisites and credits are part of the LEED building rating systems, MPRs are Minimum Project Requirements, and the foundation of the LEED building rating systems is the triple bottom line, which means <u>people, profit, and planet</u>.

75. Answer: c

    The project cannot use LEED NC certification because the building is less than 4 stories high. The project team should use the LEED for Homes rating system instead.

76. Answer: d

    Per Montreal Protocol, the manufacture of HVAC units containing CFCs was stopped in the United States in 1995. These units will be phased out from existing buildings located in the United States by 2011. HCFCs, which are less active, have to be phased out by 2030.

77. Answer: b and c

    Grease typically goes down the drains in the kitchen as part of the blackwater. Toxic metal can be found in blackwater also. CO and halons are unlikely to be found in wastewater.

78. Answer: c

    Answer "a" is good practice, but is not the best choice; no matter how good a job you do, the system can still fail and leak out refrigerants. Answer "b" is partially correct; there are refrigerants without ODP (ozone depletion potential) that still have GWP (global warming potential). Answer "c" is the best choice; if you do not use refrigerants, there is absolutely no chance for them to leak out and cause environmental damage.

79. Answer: a and d
    The LEED project boundary only includes the portion of the site submitted by the project team for LEED certification, and does not necessarily overlap with the edge of the entire development, or the edge of the building. The boundary does include the entire project scope of work

80. Answer: b and d
    Reduced disturbance of wetlands is an environmental benefit, not necessarily an economic benefit. Increased use of rapidly renewable materials may not save money. Better IEQ does create fewer liabilities, lowers the cost related to employees' health, and reduces the number of employee sick days.

81. Answer: c and d
    Biofuel is generated from plant material like crops, trees, and grasses. Gas and natural gas are both fossil fuels.

82. Answer: a
    All other choices are good practice, but they do NOT necessarily need to be implemented for water efficiency.

83. Answer: a
    This is the definition of durability.

84. Answer: b and c

    The removal of refrigerants containing ODP and GWP should be conducted by a specialist, and is not part of a construction waste management plan. The reduction of building size is part of the design decision, not part of a construction waste management plan.

85. Answer: c and d

    HCFCS and CFCs should not be used because of their ozone depletion potential (ODP).

86. Answer: d

    Answer "b" can earn points for Exemplary Performance, not for Innovation in Design.

87. Answer: c

    The same strategy can be used for other projects, but it may or may not earn an ID point. Each case has to be reviewed and determined by GBCI.

88. Answer: b

    NH3 has a lower GWP than HCFC.

    For more information, see: "**The Treatment by LEED of the Environmental Impact of HVAC Refrigerants**." You can download this PDF file for free at the link below:

http://www.gbci.org/Files/References/The-Treatment-by-LEED-of-the-Environmental-Impact-of-HVAC-Refrigerants.pdf

This is a VERY important document that you need to become familiar with. Many real LEED exam questions (CFC, HCFC, HFC, etc.) come from this document. You should download the file and read <u>at least</u> 3 times.

Pay special attention to the Table on ODP and GWP. You do not have to remember the exact value of all ODPs and GWPs, but you do need to know the rough number for various groups of refrigerants.

89. Answer: a
An educational program on LEED is the most common way to gain points under the Innovation in Design category. Answer "b" may help the project earn a higher level of LEED certification, but no other rewards. Answer "c" may earn extra points for Exemplary Performance, but not for Innovation in Design

90. Answer: a
Proper building orientation and fenestration can take full advantage of the dominant winds in the summer, and avoid chilly north winds in the winter. These characteristics can also take full advantage of passive heat-

ing from the sun in the winter, and avoid the westerly sun in the summer. This can be more efficient than ALL the HVAC equipment combined. There is no such thing as LEED certified equipment.

91. Answer: c
All LEED rating systems can have CIRs, including LEED ND.

92. Answer: b
ASHRAE standards do not apply to WE.

93. Answer: b
Rainwater is non-potable water. Please also see the definitions for blackwater and graywater in the explanations of Questions #9, #10, #32, and #67. Raw water is a distracter.

94. Answer: b
Prerequisites are the most important criteria for a LEED building rating system. They HAVE to be met before a building can earn LEED certification. Quantifiable performances, credits, and third party standards only apply to part of the LEED rating systems, and not ALL of them have to be met.

95. Answer: b and d
Hardscape can reduce landscape area; mulches can prevent moisture loss. Both can reduce water for landscape irrigation. Perennials use more water. Overhead irrigation

can increase water loss due to runoff and evaporation by the sun and wind. Head to head coverage is a standard practice for landscape irrigation.

96. Answer: a
Energy used by elevators and escalators is process energy and can be renewable energy or non-renewable energy. Non-process energy is the same as regulated energy.

The energy used by the following is considered **process energy**:
Refrigeration and kitchen cooking, laundry (washing and drying), elevators and escalators, computers, office and general miscellaneous equipment, lighting not included in the lighting power allowance (such as lighting that is part of the medical equipment), and other uses like water pumps, etc.

The energy used by the following is considered **regulated (non-process) energy**:
HVAC, exhaust fans and hood, lighting for interiors, surface parking, garage parking, building façade and grounds, space heating and service water heating, etc.

97. Answer: d
Lightweight plants are most appropriate for a vegetated roof. Native plants or adaptive plants are good for LEED projects, but some of them are NOT appropriate for rooftops. A

native tree with a large canopy on a vegetated roof means large roots will be present and may cause many problems.

98. Answer: b, d, and e
Consultation with an electrical engineer is good practice, but it is not as important as the other choices. The completion of the commissioning plan will occur AFTER on-site renewable systems are selected.

99. Answer: c
Scraps re-used from the same manufacture process, such as reground and rework, cannot be included as pre-consumer recycled items or post-consumer recycled items. Therefore, Answers "a" and "d" are incorrect. Demolition concrete pieces used at another project are salvaged materials.

100. Answer: e
The project team can ONLY advise the school board that the LEED Platinum certification is achieved after the LEED application is reviewed and APPROVED by GBCI, because the GBCI can reject the application after the review or approve the project for a lower level of LEED certification.

Chapter Two
LEED O&M Mock Exam Part II: Questions, Answers, and Explanations

I. LEED O&M Mock Exam Part II

101. A project team needs to submit a minimum of _____ of water for WEc1: Water Performance Measurement.
    a. 60%
    b. 70%
    c. 80%
    d. 90%

102. For a multitenant building, a project team needs to involve a minimum of _____ of the total gross floor space.
    a. 60%
    b. 70%
    c. 80%
    d. 90%

103. For an office building seeking LEED O&M certification, a project team needs to

address all of the following for SSc2, Building Exterior and Hardscape Management Plan except:
a. building exterior cleaning.
b. painting used on the building exterior for a detached parking garage.
c. snow and ice removal.
d. hardscape cleaning.

104. Which of the following does not have exemplary performance points? (Choose 2)
a. MRc5: Sustainable Purchasing-Food
b. MRc6: Solid Waste Management-Waste Stream Audit
c. MRc7: Solid Waste Management-Ongoing Consumables
d. MRc8: Solid Waste Management-Durable Goods

105. Which of the following are resources for Level 1 walk-through analysis? (Choose 2)
a. The *2007 ASHRAE Handbook*
b. The *Green-e manual*
c. ASHRAE *Procedures for Commercial Building Audits*
d. The *Title-24*

106. For MRc4: Sustainable Purchasing-Reduced Mercury in Lamps, the lighting purchase plan includes lamps for:
a. indoor fixtures.
b. outdoor fixtures.
c. hardwired fixtures.

d. portable fixtures.
e. All of the above

107. Which of the following are incorrect? (choose 2)
a. LEED 2009 for Existing Buildings (EB): Operation and Maintenance (O&M) addresses only the lamps purchased during the performance period, not the lamps installed in the building.
b. LEED 2009 for Existing Buildings (EB): Operation and Maintenance (O&M) addresses not only the lamps purchased during the performance period, but also the lamps installed in the building.
c. LEED 2009 O&M requires each purchased lamp comply with the specific mercury limit.
d. LEED 2009 O&M requires only the overall average of purchased lamps must comply.

108. With regard to SSc8: Light Pollution Reduction, one of the options for exterior lighting is to partially or fully shield all exterior light fixture _____watts and over so that they do not directly emit light into the night sky.
a. 50
b. 60
c. 70
d. 80

109. To earn one point for EAc3.2: Performance Measurement: System-Level Metering, a project team needs to employ system-level metering covering at least _____ of the total expected annual energy consumption of the building based on the energy-use breakdown.
   a. 20%
   b. 30%
   c. 40%
   d. 50%

110. What is the maximum number of points that a project team can earn under EAc1: Optimize Energy Performance?
   a. 16
   b. 17
   c. 18
   d. 19

111. EAp1: Energy Efficiency Best Management Practices—Planning, Documentation, and Opportunity Assessment is related to which of the following? (Choose 2)
   a. SSc7: Heat Island Reduction
   b. WEp1: Minimum Indoor Plumbing Fitting and Fitting Efficiency
   c. IEQc1: Indoor Air Quality Best Management Practices
   d. IEQc3: Green Cleaning

112. Which of the following is not eligible for

Energy Star Ratings?
a. Factory
b. Courthouse
c. Hospital
d. Warehouse

113. For the case of Mechanical Ventilation Systems under IEQc1.2: Indoor Air Quality and Quality Best Management Practices: Outdoor Air Delivery Monitoring, a design team needs to provide a device capable of measuring the minimum outdoor airflow rate within _____ of the design minimum outdoor air rate.
a. 10%
b. 15%
c. 20%
d. 25%

114. For MRc6: Solid Waste Management-Waste Stream Audit, a project team would audit:
a. cardboard being sent to an incinerator, landfill, or recycling facility
b. cardboard being sent to an incinerator, landfill, composting, or recycling facility
c. cardboard being sent to a composting or recycling facility
d. cardboard being sent to an incinerator or landfill

115. For EAc3.2: Performance and Measurement: System-Level Metering, which of the

following is not acceptable?
a. Permanent metering and recording systems
b. Metering and recording systems that operate continuously
c. Metering and recording systems that operate automatically
d. Metering and recording systems that operate electronically
e. Manual metering reading

116. For green cleaning, vacuums shall be certified by:
a. "Green Label" testing program.
b. "Green-e" testing program.
c. "Seal of Approval program" testing program.
d. EPA.

117. With regard to WEc2: Additional Indoor Plumbing Fixture and Fitting Efficiency, how many points can a project team earn if the indoor potable water use is reduced by 30%?
a. 2
b. 3
c. 4
d. 5

118. Which of the following is incorrect with regard to EAc2.2: Existing Building Commissioning: Implementation?
a. Implement low- or no-cost operations

improvements.
b. Implement all upgrades or retrofit for energy-using systems.
c. Provide training for management staff.
d. Update the building operating plan.

119. Which of the following are incorrect with regard to EAc2.3: Existing Building Commissioning: Ongoing Commissioning? (Choose 2)
   a. Only work completed within 2 years prior to application may be included to show progress in the ongoing commissioning cycle.
   b. Only work completed within 1 year prior to application may be included to show progress in the ongoing commissioning cycle.
   c. Ongoing commissioning includes BAS trend log diagnostics.
   d. Ongoing commissioning is generally undertaken simultaneously with a full retro-commissioning.

120. Which of the following can a project team use to show compliance with IEQc1.3: Indoor Air Quality Best Management Practices: Increased Ventilation? (Choose 2)
   a. Use calculations and diagrams to show the design of the natural ventilation systems meet the recommendations set forth in CIBSE.
   b. Use calculations and diagrams to show

the design of the natural ventilation systems meet the recommendations set forth in ASHRAE 52.2-1999.
   c. Use a Multizone, analytic, macroscopic model to predict that room-by-room airflows will ventilate per ASHRAE62.1-2007 for a minimum of 80% of occupied space.
   d. Use a Multizone, analytic, macroscopic model to predict that room-by-room airflows will ventilate per ASHRAE62.1-2007 for a minimum of 90% of occupied space.

121. Which of the following can be exempt from the requirements of Natural Ventilation systems of IEQc1.2: Indoor Air Quality and Quality Best Management Practices: Outdoor Air Delivery Monitoring? (Choose 2)
   a. Rooms smaller than 100 sf
   b. If the total area of all naturally ventilated spaces is less than 5% of the area of the total occupied spaces
   c. Small conference rooms
   d. Workstations in an open office

122. Wood products designated as FSC Recycled are:
   a. recycled content.
   b. recycled materials.
   c. diverted materials.
   d. FSC-certified wood.

123. How many levels of cleanliness do the APPA's 1992 Custodial Staffing Guidelines include?
   a. 3
   b. 4
   c. 5
   d. 6

124. For a multitenant building, a project seeking LEED O&M certification must:
   a. involve a minimum of 90% of the total gross floor area
   b. involve a minimum of 90% of the total gross floor area and 90% of the tenant spaces
   c. involve a minimum of 80% of the total gross floor area
   d. involve a minimum of 80% of the total gross floor area and 80% of the tenant spaces

125. All of the following affect the targeted level of weighted average mercury content in lamps except: (Choose 2)
   a. colors.
   b. life span of lamps.
   c. lumen output.
   d. lamp types.

126. For LEED O&M, the baseline water use is determined by:
   a. the year of substantial completion.
   b. the year when 100% of the building is

completely finished.
c. the year when the Certificate of Occupancy is issued.
d. the year when at least 90% of the plumbing fixtures and fittings are retrofitted.

127. When calculating stormwater runoff volumes using the rational method, the following areas shall be included except:
a. roof.
b. pavement.
c. surface waters.
d. turf.

128. With regard to IEQ Credit 1.4 IAQ Best Management Practices: Reduce Particulates in Air Distribution, what is the minimum MERV for the filtration media that a project uses for inside air recirculation and outside air intake?
a. 8
b. 13
c. 15
d. 17

129. Which of the following is not related to chemical management of the cooling tower?
a. Bleed-off
b. Condensation
c. Biological control
d. Staff management

130. What is EPA's I-BEAM related to?

a. Integrated pest management
b. Indoor Building Environment Air Management
c. Emission reduction
d. Light pollution reduction
e. Indoor Air Quality Building Education and Assessment Model

131. A power company helps a project team build an on-site solar energy system and retains the environmental attributes. Which of the following is true?
    a. This solar system cannot earn points for EAc4: On-Site and Off-Site Renewable Energy.
    b. The owner can use net-metering for this system to earn credit.
    c. This solar system can earn RECs.
    d. None of the above

132. Visible light transmittance is related to which of the following?
    a. Albedo
    b. SRI
    c. Light pollution control
    d. Daylighting

133. Which of the following is not source reduction?
    a. Ordering the correct quantity and grade of concrete
    b. Protect construction materials from weather damages

c. Recycling extra gypsum boards
d. Order the right quantity of equipment

134. The length of the building entrance grate system should be:
    a. 6 feet placed at the exterior of the building.
    b. 10 feet placed at the exterior of the building.
    c. 6 feet placed at the interior of the building.
    d. 10 feet placed at the interior of the building.

135. The landscape management plan addresses the following operational elements except:
    a. IPM.
    b. EPA.
    c. diversion of landscape waste.
    d. erosion and sedimentation control.

136. How much of the total combined food and beverage purchases must be sustainable purchase to earn MRc5: Sustainable Purchase: Food?
    a. 15%
    b. 20%
    c. 25%
    d. 30%

137. Which of the following are true regarding MRc3: Sustainable Purchasing: Facility Alterations and Additions?

a. It only includes building elements permanently attached to the building.
b. It includes materials and labor costs.
c. It includes furniture, fixtures, and equipment (FF&E).
d. It excludes MEP components and elevators.

138. What is bleed-off?
    a. It is the process of releasing a portion of the evaporating water from the cooling tower.
    b. It is the process of draining a portion of the re-circulating water from the cooling tower.
    c. It is the process of adding chemicals to the water used in the cooling tower.
    d. None of the above

139. What is the advantage of chemical treatment in cooling towers? (Choose 3)
    a. Reduces the use of potable water
    b. Reduces evaporation
    c. Stronger cooling power
    d. Controls mineral deposits
    e. Prevents the outbreak of Legionella pneumophila

140. With regard to WEc1: Water Performance Measurement, what percent of the irrigated landscape area must be included in sub-metering?
    a. 70%

b. 80%
c. 90%
d. 100%

141. How can points be earned for WEc3: Water Efficient Landscaping?
    a. Show water use reduction by comparing the actual water use by landscape irrigation against the baseline.
    b. Install sub-metering for at least 60% of the landscape area.
    c. Install sub-metering for at least 80% of the landscape area.
    d. Use ANSI irrigation performance and ranking tools to show compliance.

142. Which of the following is not related to WEc1: Water Performance Measurement?
    a. Metering
    b. Sub-metering
    c. Process water
    d. Irrigation
    e. None of the above

143. Which of the following credit category is related to ENERGY STAR products?
    a. SS
    b. EA
    c. MR
    d. IEQ

144. Which of the following can help earn SSc8: Light Pollution Reduction for LEED

O&M? (Choose 2)
a. Partially shield 60% of all light fixtures to prevent emitting light into the night sky.
b. Meeting SSc8 requirements under LEED NC or Schools to prevent emitting light to the night sky.
c. All light fixtures should be at least 50% partially shielded to prevent emitting light into the night sky.
d. Install a monitoring system.

145. Which of the following are not required to earn EAc2.3: Existing Building Commissioning: Ongoing Commissioning? (Choose 2)
a. Complete at least 50% of the scope of the work before submitting the application for LEED O&M.
b. Complete 100% of the scope of the work before submitting the application for LEED O&M.
c. Use only actual costs to document completed tasks.
d. Use actual costs or estimated costs to document completed tasks.

146. Which of the following are not related to BAS? (Choose 2)
a. DDC
b. Occupancy sensors
c. Controlled devices
d. Time clock

e. Setpoints and setbacks

147. How many point(s) will a project earn if it has in place an Environmentally Preferable Purchasing (EPP) Policy?
    a. 0
    b. 1
    c. 2
    d. 3

148. In an office building where the tenant turnover rate is high, what is a good strategy to achieve MRc2: Sustainable Purchasing: Durable Goods?
    a. A furniture salvage program
    b. Selling used furniture to recycled facilities
    c. Buying only furniture with pre- and postconsumer content
    d. RECs
    e. Green Seal program

149. All typical HVAC equipment is assumed to have a life of:
    a. 15 years
    b. 20 years
    c. 25 years
    d. 30 years

150. What is the maximum number of points that a project can earn for exemplary performance under IOc1: Innovation in Operations?

a. 2
b. 3
c. 4
d. 5

151. A project team must document the following in writing for Innovation in Operations except: (Choose 3)
    a. intent.
    b. definition.
    c. strategies.
    d. performance metric.
    e. reference codes.

152. Which of the following changes will affect building operating plan updates? (Choose 3)
    a. Lighting level
    b. Equipment run-time schedule
    c. Sustainable purchase
    d. Occupancy schedule
    e. Solid waste management

153. If a project is certified under LEED O&M, how often can the project be recertified?
    a. Every year
    b. Every 2 years
    c. Every 3 years
    d. Every 4 years
    e. Every 5 years

154. What is the maximum gap within a performance period?
    a. 1 day

b. 1 week
c. 1 month
d. 1 year

155. With regard to IEQc2.1: Occupant Comfort: Occupant Survey, what percentage of occupants must be included in the occupant comfort survey?
   a. 30%
   b. 60%
   c. 80%
   d. 90%

156. Which of the following are not a type of structural control for controlling erosion and sedimentation? (Choose 2)
   a. Silt fencing
   b. Mulching
   c. Catch basin
   d. Earth dike

157. Which of the following are not types of non-potable water that can be used for WEc4: Cooling Tower Water Management? (Choose 2)
   a. Swimming pool filter backwash water
   b. Recycled treated wastewater from toilet and urinal flushing
   c. Naturally occurring groundwater
   d. Surface water

158. A building operation plan is also called:
   a. owner's operating requirements.

b. developer's operating requirements.
c. tenant's operating requirements.
d. management's operating requirements.

159. With regard to a cooling tower, which of the following can help to prevent exposure to Legionella pneumophila? (Choose 2)
   a. The use of non-potable water
   b. Biocides
   c. Reducing evaporation
   d. Well-maintained drift eliminators
   e. The use of potable water

160. With regard to EAc1: Optimize Energy Performance, what percentile level above the national median is the building if it can earn one point and is eligible for an Energy Star rating?
   a. 21%
   b. 45%
   c. 71%
   d. 95%

161. What is the minimum performance period for EAp2 and EAc1, and what is the minimum performance period for other prerequisites and credits?
   a. 9 months, 1 month
   b. 12 months, 3 months
   c. 12 months, 1 month
   d. 9 months, 3 months

162. What is the maximum performance pe-

riod?
a. 9 months
b. 12 months
c. 24 months
d. 36 months

163. With regard to EAc1: Optimize Energy Performance, what percentile level above the national median is the building if it can earn one point and is not eligible for an Energy Star rating?
a. 21%
b. 45%
c. 71%
d. 95%

164. For stormwater quantity control, a project team needs to perform all necessary stabilization, repairs, or routine required maintenance within _____ days of inspection?
a. 15
b. 30
c. 45
d. 60

165. For a naturally ventilated space, which of the following is not an acceptable way to meet the requirements of IEQc1.3: Indoor Air Quality Best Management Practices: Increased Ventilation?
a. Increase ventilation to 30% above the minimum required by ASHRAE Standard 55.2-2007.

b. Use calculations and diagrams to show the systems meet the criteria of CIBSE Applications Manual 10:2005.
c. Use a Multizone, analytical, macroscopic model to predict room-by-room airflows will meet ASHRAE Standard.
d. None of the above

166. A project team has conducted a walk-through analysis 2 years before the performance period. Which of the following are true with regard to EAp1: Energy Efficiency Best Management Practices—Planning, Documentation, and Opportunity Assessment? (Choose 2)
    a. The project team has to redo the walk-through analysis again.
    b. The project team does not have to redo the walk-through analysis again.
    c. The project team has to do an updated report.
    d. None of the above

167. Which of the following belong to operational effective credits? (Choose 2)
    a. Metering of energy use
    b. Non-potable water use
    c. Pest management methods
    d. Optimizing daylight and views

168. A $100 purchase that contains 40% post-industrial materials and 60% of the content harvested within 300 miles of the project

can be counted as _____ of sustainable purchasing?
a. $100
b. $150
c. $200
d. $300

169. How can a project meet Minimum Indoor Air Quality Performance? (Choose 2)
a. Meets ASHRAE 62.1-2007
b. Meets ASHRAE 90.1-2007
c. Supplies at least 10 cubic feet per minute per person of outdoor air
d. Supplies at least 20 cubic feet per minute per person of outdoor air

170. Which of the following are not the I-BEAM protocols form managing major sources of pollution in buildings? (Choose 2)
a. Shipping and receiving
b. Using filters with proper MERV
c. Pest control
d. Entry grates with sufficient length
e. Painting
f. Remodeling and renovation

171. Which of the following are strategies for promoting hand hygiene and comply with green cleaning policy? (Choose 2)
a. Use hand soaps with antimicrobial agents if allowed by codes.
b. Use hand soaps without antimicrobial

agents if allowed by codes.
c. Use hand paper towels with recycled content.
d. Use waterless hand sanitizers.

172. A project team has done an O&M Occupant Commute Survey, and only 70% of the regular building occupants responded. Which of the following is true?
    a. This survey is not valid because it has not reached the minimum percentage required.
    b. The non-respondents are considered as solo drivers.
    c. The project can extrapolate the commuting behavior of the respondents to non-respondents.
    d. None of the above

173. With regard to Performance Measurement: System-Level Metering, how often must the project team compile summaries of results for each system covered?
    a. Daily and monthly
    b. Monthly and yearly
    c. Monthly
    d. Yearly

174. With regard to light pollution reduction, if the top of a window glass is 8 feet from the floor, what is the exempt distance from the window for an interior light that is above the top of the window glass?

a. 4 feet
b. 8 feet
c. 12 feet
d. 16 feet

175. With regard to the building exterior and hardscape management plan, which of the following are less environmentally friendly ways of snow and ice removal? (Choose 2)
a. Calcium chloride
b. Magnesium chloride
c. Potassium acetate
d. Sodium chloride

176. How should the energy-use intensity be calculated?
a. Total kBtu/Gross Floor Area
b. Total kw/Gross Floor Area
c. Total Energy Cost/Gross Floor Area
d. (Total Energy Cost + Total Water Cost)/Gross Floor Area

177. What is the intent of ASHRAE Level walk-through?
a. To conduct an energy audit
b. To check and adjust BAS
c. To check and adjust the lighting system
d. To check and adjust the HVAC system

178. If a project is not eligible for an Energy Star Rating, it must be _____ more energy efficient than the average of similar types of buildings in the nation to qualify for LEED

O&M certification.
a. 21%
b. 19%
c. 17%
d. 15%

179. Which of the following lists each distinct type of system, such as humidification, dehumidification, ventilation, space cooling, etc?
a. Building operating plan
b. Preventive maintenance plan
c. Sequence of operations
d. Systems narrative

180. Which of the following are ineligible on-site renewable systems? (Choose 3)
a. Photovoltaic
b. Passive solar strategies
c. Animal waste
d. Landfill gas
e. Daylighting strategies
f. Geoexchange systems

181. How many points can a project earn for exemplary performance under IOc1: Innovation in Operation?
a. 1
b. 2
c. 3
d. 4

182. How many points can a project earn for

RPc1: Regional Priority?
a. 3
b. 4
c. 5
d. 6

183. If a project's site area is 1 acre and the building footprint is 10,000 sf, how much of the off-site areas need to be covered with adapted or native plants for the project to earn 1 point for SSc5: Site Development: Protect or Restore Open Habitat?
a. 2,500 sf
b. 5,000 sf
c. 10,000 sf
d. 21,780 sf

184. What is CIBSE Application Manual related to?
a. BMP
b. Energy audit
c. Air conditioning
d. Ventilation
e. Lighting

185. Which of the following must a detailed plan for ongoing commissioning include? (Choose 3)
a. Maintenance tasks
b. System testing
c. Operation schedule
d. Corrective action
e. Measurements

186. Which of the following are true? (Choose 2)
   a. A project must have an Energy Star Rating of 71 or higher to earn an Energy Star Label.
   b. A project must have an Energy Star Rating of 75 or higher to earn an Energy Star Label.
   c. A project that is not eligible for an Energy Star Label can earn LEED certification.
   d. A project that is not eligible for an Energy Star Label cannot earn LEED certification.

187. In an unincorporated area with no codes regarding erosion control, which of the following shall a project team follow?
   a. CPESC
   b. EPA's Stormwater Pollution Prevention Plans
   c. IPM
   d. Erosion Control Technical Council

188. With regard to SSc4, Alternative Commuting Transportation includes all but which of the following?
   a. Human-powered conveyances
   b. Alternative-fuel vehicle
   c. Expanded workweeks
   d. Telecommuting

189. A vegetated roof can contribute to all but which of the following?
   a. SSc7.2: Heat Island Reduction: Roof
   b. EAc1: Optimize Energy Efficiency Performance
   c. IEQc2.4: Daylight and Views
   d. SSc5: Site Development: Protect or Restore Open Habitat

190. Which of the following is related to ASHRAE Level II Energy Audit?
   a. EAp1: Energy Efficiency Best Management Practices—Planning, Documentation, and Opportunity Assessment
   b. EAc1: Optimize Energy Efficiency Performance
   c. EAc2.1: Existing Building Commissioning: Investigations and Analysis
   d. EAc3.2: Performance Measurement: System-Level Metering

191. Which of the following tasks is not included in an ASHRAE Level II Energy Audit?
   a. A rough estimate energy-use breakdown per 1996 ASHRAE Handbook
   b. A review of the electrical and mechanical system design
   c. A list of possible modifications that can save money
   d. An estimate of the cost for each practical measure

192. Excluding skylights, photovoltaic panel, and mechanical equipment, which of the following will help a project earn an IO Exemplary Performance point?
   a. A vegetated roof that covers 95% of the roof area
   b. A vegetated roof that covers 75% of the roof area
   c. (Area of Roof Meeting Minimum SRI/Total Roof Area) x (SRI of Installed Roof/Required SRI)≥75%
   d. (Area of Roof Meeting Minimum SRI/0.75) x (SRI of Installed Roof/0.5)≥ Total Roof Area

193. With regard to SSc1: LEED Certified Design and Construction, which of the following is true?
   a. If the project has been certified under LEED NC before, it can earn 3 points.
   b. If the project has been certified under LEED School before, it can earn 2 points.
   c. If the project has been certified under LEED CS and 75% of the floor area has been certified under LEED CI before, it can earn an IO bonus point.
   d. If the project has been certified under LEED CS and 75% of the floor area has been certified under LEED CI before, it can earn 4 points.

194. Per Energy Star Rating System, what is an average building's performance?
   a. 21
   b. 45
   c. 50
   d. 71

195. With regard to EAc2.3, only work completed with _____ years prior to application may be included to show progress in the ongoing commissioning cycle
   a. 2
   b. 3
   c. 4
   d. 5

196. With regard to SSc8: Light Pollution Reduction, which of the following must be accomplished for a project to earn one point?
   a. All non-emergency lights visible from outside must be programmed to automatically turn off for at least 50% of the nighttime hours every night.
   b. The project must have earned LEED NC certification and at least 75% of the total floor area must have been certified under LEED CI.
   c. All non-emergency lights visible from outside must be programmed to automatically turn off for at least 2,190 hours per year.
   d. The exterior lighting level must be equal

to 20% or less of the interior lighting level.

197. With regard to SSc2: Building Exterior and Hardscape Management Plan, which of the following standards must the exterior sealant comply with?
    a. SCAQMD
    b. Green Seal's Standard GS-11
    c. Environmental Choice CCD-110
    d. SMACNA

198. A project team is seeking an Energy Star Rating for a building EPA allows the exclusion of up to 10% of gross floor area if: (Choose 2)
    a. the space does not fit any of the Energy Star space type classifications.
    b. the energy use of that space is estimated accurately based on similar spaces.
    c. the energy use of that space is submetered.
    d. the space is completely sealed off and separated from other spaces.

199. A project team can use _____ to relate the emissions from a building's energy consumption to the source of that energy.
    a. NERC Regions
    b. eGRID Subregions
    c. Portfolio Manager
    d. Energy Star's Portfolio Manager

200. Which of the following cannot earn exemplary performance points?
   a. SSc6: Stormwater Quantity Control
   b. SSc7.1: Heat Island Reduction: Non-roof
   c. SSc7.2: Heat Island Reduction: Roof
   d. SSc8: Light Pollution Reduction

II. Answers and Explanations for the LEED O&M Mock Exam Part II

101. Answer: c

102. Answer: d
  See LEED O&M reference guide, Introduction, Multitenant Buildings.

103. Answer: c
  Painting used on the building exterior for a <u>detached</u> parking garage.

104. Answer: b and d

105. Answer: a and c
  See LEED O&M reference guide, Summary of Reference Standards under EAp1: Energy Efficiency Best Management Practices—Planning, Documentation, and Opportunity Assessment.

106. Answer: e

See MRc4: Sustainable Purchasing-Reduced Mercury in Lamps.

107. Answer: b and c
See MRc4: Sustainable Purchasing-Reduced Mercury in Lamps.

108. Answer: a
See SSc8: Light Pollution Reduction.

109. Answer: c
See EAc3.2: Performance Measurement: System-Level Metering.

110. Answer: d
18 regular points + 1 exemplary performance point = 19 points. See EAc1: Optimize Energy Performance.

111. Answer: b and c
See EAp1: Energy Efficiency Best Management Practices—Planning, Documentation, and Opportunity Assessment.

112. Answer: a
See Implementation Section under EAc1.

113. Answer: b
See IEQc1.2: Indoor Air Quality and Quality Best Management Practices: Outdoor Air Delivery Monitoring.

114. Answer: b

See Implementation Section under MRc6: Solid Waste Management-Waste Stream Audit. Cardboard can go to an incinerator, or landfill, or composting, or recycling facility.

115. Answer: e
See Implementation Section under EAc3.2: Performance and Measurement: System-Level Metering.

116. Answer: a
See IEQc3.4: Green Cleaning: Sustainable Clean Equipment.

117. Answer: d
See WEc2: Additional Indoor Plumbing Fixture and Fitting Efficiency.

118. Answer: b
See EAc2.2: Existing Building Commissioning: Implementation. The project team needs to create a capital plan for major upgrades or retrofits, but they do not need to implement all upgrades or retrofit for energy-using systems.

119. Answer: b and d
See Requirements, Implementation, and Examples under EAc2.3: Existing Building Commissioning: Ongoing Commissioning.

120. Answer: a and d

See Requirements under IEQc1.3: Indoor Air Quality Best Management Practices: Increased Ventilation.

121. Answer: a and d
See Requirements under IEQc1.2: Indoor Air Quality and Quality Best Management Practices: Outdoor Air Delivery Monitoring.

122. Answer: a

123. Answer: c
See Summary of Reference Standards under IEQc3.2: Green Cleaning: Custodial Effectiveness Assessment.

124. Answer: a
See LEED O&M reference guide, Introduction, Multitenant Buildings.

125. Answer: a and d
See Implementation under MRc4: Sustainable Purchasing: Reduced Mercury in Lamps.

126. Answer: a
See Requirements under WEp1: Minimum Indoor Plumbing Fixture and Fitting Efficiency.

127. Answer: c
See Calculations under SSc6: Stormwater Quality Control.

128. Answer: b
See Requirements under IEQ Credit 1.4 IAQ Best Management Practices: Reduce Particulates in Air Distribution.

129. Answer: b
See Requirements under WEc4: Cooling Tower Water Management.

130. Answer: e
Answer b has some truth, but e is the best answer. See Requirements under IEQc1.1: Indoor Air Quality Best Management Practices: Indoor Air Quality Management Program.

131. Answer: a
The environmental attributes of an on-site solar energy system need to be retained on-site, instead of by the power company, to earn LEED O&M credits.

132. Answer: d
See definitions under IEQc2.4: Daylight and Views.

133. Answer: c
See Implementation under MRc9: Solid Waste Management: Facility Alterations and Additions. Source reduction is different from recycling.

134. Answer: d

See Requirements under IEQc3.5: Green Cleaning: Indoor Chemical and Pollutant Source Control.

135. Answer: b
See Requirements under SSc3: Integrated Pest Management, Erosion Control, and Landscape Management Plan.

136. Answer: c
Pay attention to the word "must." See Requirements under MRc5: Sustainable Purchase: Food.

137. Answer: d
See Requirements under MRc3: Sustainable Purchasing: Facility Alterations and Additions.

138. Answer: b
See definition under WEc4: Cooling Tower Water Management.

139. Answer: a, d, and e
See Implementation under WEc4: Cooling Tower Water Management.

140. Answer: b
See Requirements under WEc1: Water Performance Measurement.

141. Answer: a
See Requirements under WEc3: Water Effi-

cient Landscaping. Answers b and c are trying to confuse you with information for WEc1. Answer d is a made-up distracter that does not exist.

142. Answer: e
See Requirements under WEc1: Water Performance Measurement

143. Answer: c
Pay attention to the difference between ENERGY STAR <u>products</u> and ENERGY STAR <u>rating</u>: ENERGY STAR <u>products</u> are related to <u>MR</u>, but ENERGY STAR <u>rating</u> is related to <u>EA</u>.

144. Answer: b and c
See Requirements under SSc8: Light Pollution Reduction for LEED O&M.

145. Answer: b and c
See Requirements under EAc2.3: Existing Building Commissioning: Ongoing Commissioning.

146. Answer: b and d
See Implementation under EAc3.1: Performance Measurement: Building Automation System.

147. Answer: a
See MRp1 Sustainable Purchasing Policy. An Environmentally Preferable Purchasing

(EPP) Policy is a mandatory prerequisite and cannot earn any point(s).

148. Answer: a

    See Implementation under MRc2: Sustainable Purchasing: Durable Goods.

149. Answer: a

    See Calculations under EAc5: Enhanced Refrigerant Management.

150. Answer: b

    See Requirements under IOc1: Innovation in Operations.

151. Answer: b, c, and e

    See Requirements under IOc1: Innovation in Operations.

152. Answer: a, b, and d

    See Requirements under EAc2.2: Existing Building Commissioning: Implementation.

153. Answer: a

    See LEED O&M reference guide, Introduction, Part IV Initial Certification vs. Recertification. A LEED O&M project must be recertified every 5 years to maintain certification, but can be recertified every year.

154. Answer: a

    See LEED O&M reference guide, Introduction, Part VI, Performance Period.

155. Answer: a
See Requirements under IEQc2.1: Occupant Comfort: Occupant Survey.

156. Answer: b and c
See Implementation, Erosion, and Sedimentation Control under SSc3: Integrated Pest Management, Erosion Control, and Landscape Management Plan.

157. Answer: c and d
See Requirements under WEc4: Cooling Tower Water Management.

158. Answer: a
See Implementation under EAp1: Energy Efficiency Best Management Practices—Planning, Documentation, and Opportunity Assessment.

159. Answer: b and d
See Implementation under WEc4: Cooling Tower Water Management.

160. Answer: a
See Requirements, Case 1 under EAc1: Optimize Energy Performance.

161. Answer: b
See LEED O&M reference guide, Introduction, Part VI, Performance Period.

162. Answer: c

See LEED O&M reference guide, Introduction, Part VI, Performance Period.

163. Answer: a

See Requirements, Case 2 under EAc1: Optimize Energy Performance.

164. Answer: d

See Requirements under SSc6: Stormwater Quantity Control.

165. Answer: a

See Requirements under IEQc1.3: Indoor Air Quality Best Management Practices: Increased Ventilation.

166. Answer: b and c

See Implementation, Energy Audit: Walk-Through Analysis under EAp1: Energy Efficiency Best Management Practices—Planning, Documentation, and Opportunity Assessment.

167. Answer: a and b

See LEED O&M Reference Guide, Introduction, Certification Strategy.

168. Answer: c

See Requirements under MRc1: Sustainable Purchasing: Ongoing Consumables.

169. Answer: a and c

See Requirements under IEQp1: Minimum Indoor Air Quality Performance.

170. Answer: b and d
See Implementation under IEQc1.1: Indoor Air Quality Best Management Practices: Indoor Air Quality Management Program.

171. Answer: b and d
See Implementation under IEQp1: Green Cleaning Policy.

172. Answer: b
See Calculations under SSc4: Alternative Commuting Transportation. The non-respondents are considered as solo drivers, and the project cannot extrapolate the commuting behavior of the respondents to non-respondents unless the response rate is 80% or more of the regular building occupants.

173. Answer: b
See Requirements under EAc3.2: Performance Measurement: System-Level Metering.

174. Answer: c
See Implementation under SSc8: Light Pollution Reduction.

175. Answer: a and d
See Implementation under SSc2: Building Exterior and Hardscape Management Plan.

176. Answer: a

See Calculations under EAp1: Energy Efficiency Best Management Practices—Planning, Documentation, and Opportunity Assessment.

177. Answer: a

See Requirements under EAp1: Energy Efficiency Best Management Practices—Planning, Documentation, and Opportunity Assessment.

178. Answer: a

See Requirements under EAp2: Minimum Energy Efficiency Performance. Please note this is different from the 21% required by EAc1.

179. Answer: d

See Implementation under EAp1: Energy Efficiency Best Management Practices—Planning, Documentation, and Opportunity Assessment.

180. Answer: b, e, and f

See Implementation under EAc4: On-Site and Off-Site Renewable Energy.

181. Answer: c

See Requirements under IOc1: Innovation in Operation.

182. Answer: b
   See Requirements under RPc1: Regional Priority.

183. Answer: d
   See Requirements under SSc5: Site Development: Protect or Restore Open Habitat.

   The building footprint (10,000 s.f) is a distracter. This question also tests your basic and common construction knowledge:
   1 acre = 43,560 sf
   25% of the site area = 50% x 43,560 sf = 10,890 sf

   Because every 2 sf of off-site area covered with adapted or native plants equals 1 sf on-site, the off-site area needed = 2 x 10,890 sf = 21,780 sf

184. Answer: d
   See Requirements under IEQc1.3: Indoor Air Quality Best Management Practices: Increased Ventilation.

185. Answer: b, d, and e
   See Implementation under EAc2.3: Existing Building Commissioning: Ongoing Commissioning.

186. Answer: b and c
   See Implementation under EAc1: Optimize Energy Performance.

187. Answer: b

See Implementation under SSc3: Integrated Pest Management, Erosion Control, and Landscape Management Plan.

188. Answer: c

See Requirements under SSc4: Alternative Commuting Transportation. Pay attention to the word "but."

189. Answer: c

See related credit under SSc7.2: Heat Island Reduction: Roof.

190. Answer: c

See Requirements under EAc2.1: Existing Building Commissioning: Investigations and Analysis.

191. Answer: a

See Implementation under EAc2.1: Existing Building Commissioning: Investigations and Analysis. It is per the 1999 ASHRAE Handbook, NOT the 1996 ASHRAE Handbook.

192. Answer: c

See Exemplary Performance under SSc7.2: Heat Island Reduction: Roof.

193. Answer: d

See Requirements and Exemplary Performance under SSc1: LEED Certified Design and Construction. There is no bonus point for SSc1. This is a trick to confuse you. If you firmly understand and master the LEED O&M system, you will do fine in the real exam.

194. Answer: c

See Energy Star definition.

195. Answer: a

See Requirements under EAc2.3: Existing Building Commissioning: Ongoing Commissioning.

196. Answer: c

See Requirements under SSc8: Light Pollution Reduction. Pay attention to the word "must."

All non-emergency lights visible from outside must be programmed to automatically turn off for at least 2,190 hours per year, NOT 50% of the nighttime hours <u>every night</u>.

The project must have earned LEED NC <u>OR LEED for School</u> certification, and at least 75% of the total floor area must have been certified under LEED CI.

197. Answer: a

See Implementation under SSc2: Building Exterior and Hardscape Management Plan.

198. Answer: a and c
See Implementation under EAc1: Optimize Energy Performance.

199. Answer: b
See Regional Variations under EAc6: Emissions Reduction Reporting.

200. Answer: d
See LEED O&M Reference Guide, Introduction, X. Exemplary Performance Strategies.

III. How was the LEED O&M Mock Exam created?

I tried to be scientific when selecting the mock exam questions, so I based the number of questions for each credit category roughly on the number of points that you can get for that category, otherwise known as LEED Credit Weighting. See the detailed discussion below. The difficulty level for each question was designed to match the 12 sample questions that can be downloaded from the official GBCI Web site.

If you answered 60% of the questions correctly for each part, you have passed the mock exam.

IV. Latest trend for LEED exams

Recently, some readers have encountered versions of the LEED exams that contain many questions on refrigerants (CFC, HCFC, and HFC). The following advice will help you answer these questions correctly:

For more information, download the free PDF file called "The Treatment by LEED of the Environmental Impact of HVAC Refrigerants" at the following link:

http://www.gbci.org/Files/References/The-Treatment-by-LEED-of-the-Environmental-Impact-of-HVAC-Refrigerants.pdf

This is a VERY important document that you need to become familiar with. Many real LEED exam questions (CFC, HCFC, HFC, etc.) come from this document. Be familiar with this material.

Pay special attention to the table on ODP and GWP on page 3. You do not have to remember the exact value of all ODPs and GWPs, but you do need to know the rough numbers for various groups of refrigerants.

This latest trend regarding refrigerants (CFC, HCFC, and HFC) for LEED Exams has much to do with LEED v3.0 Credit Weighting. EA (including refrigerants) is the biggest winner in LEED v3.0, meaning the category has MORE questions than any other areas for ALL the LEED exams. See pages 36 to 38 of my book, *LEED GA Exam Guide* quoted below:

How are LEED credits allocated and weighted?

Answer: They are allocated and weighted per strategies that will have a greater positive impact on the most important environmental factors: CO2 reductions and energy efficiency.

*They are weighted against **13 aftereffects of human activities**, including carbon footprint/climate change (25%), indoor-air quality (15%), resource/fossil-fuel depletion (9%), particulates (8%), water use/water intake (7%), human health: cancer (7%), ecotoxity (6%), eutrophication (5%), land use/habitat alteration (5%), human health: non-cancer (4%), smog formation (4%), acidification (3%), and ozone depletion (2%).*

*These 13 aftereffects were created by the U.S. Environmental Protection Agency (**EPA**), and are also known as "**TRACI**," a **mnemonic** for "Tool for the Reduction and Assessment of Chemical and Other Environmental Impacts."*

1) The USGBC used a reference building to estimate environmental impact in the 13 categories above.

2) The USGBC also used a tool developed by the

*National Institute of Standard and Technology (**NIST**) to prioritize the TRACI categories.*

3) The USGBC also created a matrix to show the existing LEED credits and the TRACI categories and used data that quantify building impacts on human health and environment to allocate points for each credit.

The points for Energy and Transportation credits have been greatly increased in LEED 2009, primarily because of the importance to reduce carbon or greenhouse gas emissions. Water Efficiency is also a big winner in the credits, doubling from 5 to 10 points for some LEED rating systems.

In addition to the weighting exercise, the USGBC also used value judgments, because if they only used the TRACI-NIST tool, some existing credits would be worth almost nothing, like the categories for human health and indoor air quality. The USGBC wanted to keep the LEED system somewhat consistent and retained the existing credits, including those with few environmental benefits. So each credit was assigned at least one point in the new system.

There are NO negative values or fractions for LEED points.

20% reduction of indoor water-use used to be able to gain points, now this is a prerequisite in LEED 2009.

V. Where can I find the latest official sample questions for the LEED O&M Exam?

Answer: You can find them, as well as the exam content, from the candidate handbook, at: http://www.gbci.org/main-nav/professional-credentials/resources/candidate-handbooks.aspx.

VI. LEED O&M Exam registration

1. How do I register for the LEED O&M Exam?

Answer: Per the GBCI, you must create an Eligibility ID at www.GBCI.org. Select the "Schedule an Exam" menu to set up an exam time and date with Prometric. You can reschedule or cancel the LEED AP Operations + Maintenance (O+M) Exam at www.prometric.com/gbci with your Prometric-issued confirmation number for the exam. You need to bring two forms of ID to the exam site. See www.prometric/gbci for a list of exam sites. Call 1-800-795-1747 (within the United States) or 202-742-3792 (outside of the United States) or e-mail exam@gbci.org if you have any questions.

2. Important Note:

You can download the "LEED AP Operations + Maintenance Exam Candidate Handbook" from the GBCI Web site for information on all the latest details and procedures. Ideally, you should download and carefully read this handbook at least three weeks before your exam.

Make sure you download and **peruse** all the free documents listed in the candidate handbook. The information will be on the test.

See the link below:

http://www.gbci.org/main-nav/professional-credentials/resources/candidate-handbooks.aspx

Chapter Three
Frequently Asked Questions (FAQ) and Other Useful Resources

The following are readers' questions, my responses, and some tips on how to pass the LEED exam on the first try and in one week:

1. **I found the reference guide way too tedious. Can I read only your books and just refer to the USGBC reference guide (if one is available for the exam I am taking) when needed?**

   Response: Yes, for LEED GA Exam or Part I of the LEED AP O+M Exam, my books are sufficient. That is one way to study. If you read only *LEED GA Exam Guide*, you already have a very good chance of passing the LEED GA Exam.

   For Part II of the LEED AP O+M Exam, we suggest you still need to read the USGBC O&M reference guide, but you do NOT have to read it from cover to cover. Read and focus on the important sections. *LEED O&M Mock Exam* will help you focus on the most important materials in the reference guide, such as prerequisites and credits intent, requirements, synergy, implementation, important equations or formulas under calculations section, etc.

LEED O&M Mock Exam will also help you become more familiar with the way that questions are asked in the real LEED O&M Exam, giving you more confidence and increasing your chance of passing.

2. Is one week really enough time for me to prepare for the exam while I am working?

Response: Yes, if you can put in 40 to 60 hours of study time during the week, you can pass the exam. This exam is similar to a history or political science exam; you need to MEMORIZE the information. If you wait too long to take the test after studying, you will probably forget much of the information.

In my book, *LEED GA Exam Guide*, I provide tips on how to MEMORIZE the information, and I have already highlighted/underlined the most important materials that you definitely have to MEMORIZE in order to pass Part I of the LEED O&M Exam. The purpose of this book is to help you to pass the LEED O&M Exam with minimum time and effort. It's designed to make your life easier.

However, to be on the safe side, for the average reader, I recommend not less than 2 weeks, but not MORE than 2 months of prep time.

3. Would you say that if I buy books from your LEED Exam Guide series, I could pass the exam without any other study materials? The books sold on the USGBC Web site cost hundreds of dollars, so I would be quite happy if I could buy your books and only use them.

Response: First of all, there are readers who have passed a LEED exam by reading only my books (www.ArchiteG.com). My goal is to write one book for each of the LEED exams and make each of my books stand alone to prepare people for one specific LEED exam.

Second, people learn in many different ways. That is why I published *LEED O&M Mock Exam* and added some new advice below for people who learn better by doing practice tests.

If you do the following things, you have a very good chance of passing the LEED exam. (However, this is NOT a guarantee; nobody can guarantee you will pass.):

a. If you study, understand, and MEMORIZE all of the information in my book, *LEED GA Exam Guide*, do NOT panic when you run into questions you are unfamiliar with. Use the guess strategy explained in my books, then you have a very good chance of passing Part I of the LEED O&M Exam.

You need to UNDERSTAND and MEMORIZE

the information in *LEED GA Exam Guide* and achieve an almost perfect score on the mock exam in order to pass the LEED GA exam or the first part of any AP exam. For the second part of the specific LEED AP exam you are taking, the corresponding book from my LEED Exam Guide series will give you the MAJORITY of the most CURRENT information that you need. You HAVE to know the information included in my book related to the specific AP Exam you are taking in order to pass the second part of the AP Exam.

b. If you have not been involved in any LEED projects before, I suggest you also go to the USGBC Web site, and download the latest LEED credit templates for the LEED rating system related to the LEED exam you are taking. Read the templates and become familiar with them. This is important. See the link below:

http://www.usgbc.org/DisplayPage.aspx?CMSPageID=222

c. In fact, some of my readers have passed the LEED Green Associate Exam with a high score by reading only my books, *LEED GA Exam Guide* and *LEED GA Mock Exams,* and WITHOUT reading the USGBC reference guide AT ALL.

The LEED exam is NOT an easy exam, but anyone with a seventh-grade education should be able to study and pass the LEED exam if s/he prepares correctly.

Since I have not published the LEED O&M Exam Guide yet, I would suggest you read the USGBC O&M reference guide. You should know what information to focus on after you read this book.

4. I am preparing for the LEED exam. Do I need to read the 2-inch thick reference guide?

Response: See the answer above.

5. For LEED v3.0, will the total number of points be more than 110 if a project receives all of the standard and extra credits?

Response: No, for LEED v3.0, there are 100 base points and 10 possible bonus points. There are many ways to achieve bonus points (extra credits or exemplary performance), but you can have a maximum number of only 6 ID and 4 Regional Priority bonus points. So, the maximum points for ANY project will be 110.

On another note, the older versions of LEED rating systems all have less than 110 possible points except LEED for **Homes**, which has 136 possible points.

6. For the exam, do I need to know the project phase in which a specific prerequisite/credit takes place? That is, pre-design, schematic design, etc.

Response: The information on the project phase (NOT LEED submittal phase) for each prerequisite/credit is NOT mentioned in the USGBC reference guides, but it is covered in the USGBC workshops. If this information is important enough for the USGBC workshops to cover, then it may show up on the actual LEED exam.

Most, if not all, other third-party books completely miss this important information. I cover the material for each prerequisite/credit in my guide book because I think it is very important.

Some people THINK that the LEED exam ONLY tests information covered by the USGBC reference guides. They are wrong.

The LEED exam does test information NOT covered by the USGBC reference guides. This may include the process of LEED submittal and project team coordination, etc.

I would MEMORIZE this information if I were you, because it may show up on the LEED exam. Besides, this information is not hard to memorize once you understand the content, and you need to know it to do actual LEED submittal work anyway.

7. **Are you writing any other books for the new LEED exams? If so, what are they?**

Response: Yes, I am working on other books in the LEED Exam Guide series. I will be writing one book for each of the LEED exams. See LEEDSeries.com for more information.

8. **Important documents that you need to download for <u>free</u>, become familiar with, and <u>memorize</u>:**

Note: GBCI and USGBC occasionally change the links to their documents, so, by the time you read this book, they may have changed some of the following links. You can simply go to their main Web site, search for the document by name, and find the most current link. You can use the same technique to search for documents by other organizations.

The main Web site for GBCI is:
http://www.gbci.org/

The main Web site for USGBC is:
http://www.usgbc.org/

a. **Every** LEED exam **tests** Credit Interpretation Request/Rulings (CIR). Download the related document, read, and <u>memorize</u>:
http://www.gbci.org/Certification/Resources/cirs.aspx

b. **Every** LEED exam **tests** project team coordination. Download *Sustainable Building Technical Manual: Part II,* by Anthony Bernheim and William Reed (1996), read, and <u>memorize</u>:
http://www.gbci.org/Files/References/Sustainable-Building-Technical-Manual-Part-II.pdf

c. Project Registration Application and LEED Certification Process:
http://www.usgbc.org/DisplayPage.aspx?CMSPageID=1497

d. LEED Online:
http://www.gbci.org/main-nav/building-certification/leed-online/about-leed-online.aspx

9. Important documents that you need to download for <u>free</u>, and become <u>familiar</u> with:

a. *LEED for Operations and Maintenance Reference Guide—Introduction* (U.S. Green Building Council, 2008):
https://www.usgbc.org/ShowFile.aspx?DocumentID=4512

b. *LEED for Operations and Maintenance Reference Guide—Glossary* (U.S. Green Building Council, 2008):
http://www.gbci.org/Files/References/LEED-for-Operations-and-Maintenance-Reference-Guide-Glossary.pdf

c. *LEED for Homes Rating System* (U.S. Green Building Council, 2008):
http://www.gbci.org/Files/References/LEED-for-Homes-Rating-System.pdf

Pay special attention to the list of **abbreviations and acronyms** on pages 105–106 and the helpful **glossary of terms** on pages 107–114.

d. *Cost of Green Revisited,* by Davis Langdon (2007):
http://www.gbci.org/Files/References/Cost-of-Green-Revisited.pdf

e. *The Treatment by LEED® of the Environmental Impact of HVAC Refrigerants* (LEED Technical and Scientific Advisory Committee, 2004):
http://www.gbci.org/Files/References/The-Treatment-by-LEED-of-the-Environmental-Impact-of-HVAC-Refrigerants.pdf

f. *Guidance on Innovation and Design (ID) Credits* (U.S. Green Building Council, 2004):
http://www.gbci.org/Files/References/Guidance-on-Innovation-and-Design-Credits.pdf

10. Do I need to take many practice questions to prepare for a LEED exam?

Response: There is NO absolutely correct answer to this question. People learn in many different ways. Personally, I am NOT crazy about doing many practice questions. Consider if you do 700 practice questions, not only must you read them all, but each question has at least 4 choices. That totals to at least 2,800 choices, which is a great deal of reading. I have seen some third-party materials that have 1,200 practice questions. That will require even MORE time to go over the materials.

I prefer to spend most of my time reading, digesting, and really understanding the fundamental materials, and MEMORIZE them naturally by re-reading the materials multiple times. This is because the fundamental materials for ANY exam will NOT change, and the scope of the exam will NOT change for the same main version of the test (until the exam moves to the next advanced version). However, there are many ways to ask you questions.

If you have a limited amount of time for preparation, it is more efficient for you to focus on the fundamental materials and actually <u>master</u> the knowledge that GBCI wants you to learn. If you can do that, then no matter how GBCI changes the exam format or how GBCI asks the questions, you will do fine in the exam.

Strategy 101 for the LEED O&M Exam is that you must recognize that you have only a limited amount of time to prepare for the exam. Therefore, you must concentrate on the most important contents of the LEED O&M Exam.

The key to passing the LEED O&M Exam, or any other exam, is to know the scope of the exam, and not to read too many books. Select one or two helpful books and focus on them. You must understand the content and memorize it. For your convenience, I have underlined the fundamental information that I think is very important. You definitely need to memorize all the information that I have underlined. You should try to understand the content first, and then memorize the content of the book by rereading it. This is a much better way than "mechanical" memory without understanding.

Most people fail the exam NOT because they are unable to answer the few "advanced" questions on the exam, but because they have read the information but can NOT recall it on the day of the exam. They spend too much time preparing for the exam, drag the preparation process on too long, seek too much information, go to too many Web sites, do too many practice questions and too many mock exams (one or two sets of mock exams are probably sufficient), and spread themselves too thin. They end up missing out on the most important information of the LEED exam, and they will fail.

To me, Memorization and Understanding work hand-in-hand. Understanding always comes first. If you really understand something, then Memorization is easy.

For example, I'll read a book's first chapter very slowly but make sure I really understand everything in it, no matter how long it takes. I do NOT care if others are faster readers than I. Then, I reread the first chapter again. This time, the reading is so much easier, and I can read it much faster. Then I try to retell the contents, focusing on substance, not the format or any particular order of things. This is a very good way for me to understand and digest the material, while <u>absorbing</u> and <u>memorizing</u> the content..

I then repeat the same procedure for each chapter, and then reread the book until I take the exam. This achieves two purposes:

1. I keep reinforcing the important materials that I already have memorized and fight against the human brain's natural tendency to forget things.

2. I also understand the content of the book much better by reading it multiple times.

If I were to attempt to memorize something without understanding it first, it would be very difficult for me to do so. Even if I were to memorize it, I would likely forget it quickly.

I always find doing too many practice questions too time-consuming and ineffective. I suggest doing two or three sets of practice questions but NOT seven or twelve sets.

Appendixes

1. Default occupancy factors

Occupancy	Gross sf per occupant	
	Transient Occupant	FTE
Educational, Daycare	630	105
Educational, K–12	1,300	140
Educational, Postsecondary	2,100	150
Grocery store	550	115
Hotel	1,500	700
Laboratory or R&D	400	0
Office, Medical	225	330
Office, General	250	0
Retail, General	550	130
Retail or Service (auto, financial, etc.)	600	130
Restaurant	435	95
Warehouse, Distribution	2,500	0
Warehouse, Storage	20,000	0

Note: This table is for projects (like CS) where the final occupant count is not available. If your project's occupancy factors are not listed above, you can use a comparable building to show the average gross sf per occupant for your building's use.

2. Important resources and further study materials you can download for <u>free</u>

Energy Performance of LEED® for New Construction Buildings: Final Report, by Cathy Turner and Mark Frankel (2008):
http://www.gbci.org/Files/References/Energy-Performance-of-LEED-for-New-Construction-Buildings-Final-Report.pdf

Foundations of the Leadership in Energy and Environmental Design Environmental Rating System: A Tool for Market Transformation (LEED Steering Committee, 2006):
http://www.gbci.org/Files/References/Foundations-of-the-Leadership-in-Energy-and-Environmental-Design-Environmental-Rating-System-A-Tool-for-Market-Transformation.pdf

AIA Integrated Project Delivery: A Guide (www.aia.org):
http://www.aia.org/contractdocs/AIAS077630

Review of ANSI/ASHRAE Standard 62.1-2004: Ventilation for Acceptable Indoor Air Quality, by Brian Kareis:
http://www.workplace-hygiene.com/articles/ANSI-ASHRAE-3.html

Best Practices of ISO-14021: Self-Declared Environmental Claims, by Kun-Mo Lee and Haruo Uehara (2003):

http://www.ecodesign-company.com/documents/BestPracticeISO14021.pdf

Bureau of Labor Statistics (www.bls.gov)

International Code Council (www.iccsafe.org)

Americans with Disabilities Act (ADA): Standards for Accessible Design (www.ada.gov):
http://www.ada.gov/stdspdf.htm

GSA 2003 Facilities Standards (General Services Administration, 2003):
http://www.gbci.org/Files/References/GSA-2003-facilities-standards.pdf

Guide to Purchasing Green Power (Environmental Protection Agency, 2004):
http://www.gbci.org/Files/References/Guide-to-Purchasing-Green-Power.pdf

USGBC Definitions:
https://www.usgbc.org/ShowFile.aspx?DocumentID=5744

3. Annotated bibliography

Chen, Gang. *LEED GA Exam Guide: A Must-Have for the LEED Green Associate Exam: Comprehensive Study Materials, Sample Questions, Mock Exam, Green Building LEED Certification, and Sustainability (LEEDv3.0).* Outskirts Press,

2009. This is a very comprehensive and concise book on the LEED Green Associate Exam. Some readers have passed the LEED Green Associate Exam by studying this book for 3 days.

Hubka, David, DE LEED AP. *LEED GA Practice Exams: Green Associate.* Professional Publications, Inc., 2009. This reference has 200 sample questions.

Leppo, Holly Williams, RA/CID LEED AP. *LEED Prep GA: What You Really Need to Know to Pass the LEED Green Associate Exam.* Professional Publications, Inc., 2009. This reference has a concise review of the exam subject and 100 sample questions.

4. Valuable Web sites and links

a. The Official Web sites for the U.S. Green Building Council (USGBC):
   http://www.usgbc.org/
   http://www.Greenbuild365.org

Pay special attention to the purpose of <u>LEED Online, LEED project registration, LEED certification content, LEED reference guide introductions, LEED rating systems, and checklists</u>.

You can download or purchase the following useful documents from the USGBC or GBCI Web site:

Latest and official LEED exam candidate handbooks including an exam content outline and sample questions:
http://www.gbci.org/main-nav/professional-credentials/resources/candidate-handbooks.aspx

LEED Reference Guides:
http://www.usgbc.org/DisplayPage.aspx?CMSPageID=2059

LEED Rating System Selection Policy:
http://www.usgbc.org/ShowFile.aspx?DocumentID=6667

Read the above document <u>at least three times</u>, because it is VERY important, and it tells you which LEED system to use.

LEED 2009 Vision and Executive Summary:
http://www.usgbc.org/ShowFile.aspx?DocumentID=4121

Various versions of LEED Green Building Rating Systems and Project Checklist:
http://www.usgbc.org/DisplayPage.aspx?CMSPageID=2059

b. Natural Resources Defense Council:
http://www.nrdc.org/

c. Environmental Construction + Design - Green Book (Offers print magazine and online environmental products and services resources guide):
http://www.edcmag.com/greenbook

d. Cool Roof Rating Council Web site:
http://www.coolroofs.org

Back Page Promotion

Other useful books written by Gang Chen:

1. *Architectural Practice Simplified: A Survival Guide and Checklists for Building Construction and Site Improvements as well as Tips on Architecture, Building Design, Construction and Project Management* (Published December 23, 2009)

2. *Planting Design Illustrated: A Must-Have for Landscape Architecture: A Holistic Garden Design Guide with Architectural and Horticultural Insight, and Ideas from Famous Gardens in Major Civilizations* (2nd edition):
http://outskirtspress.com/agent.php?key=11011&page=plantingdesignillustrated

3. **LEED Exam Guide series.** Refer to the links below:
http://www.GreenExamEducation.com
http://www.ArchiteG.com

Note: Other books in the LEED Exam Guide series are currently in production. One book will eventually be produced for each of the LEED exams. The series includes:

LEED AP EXAM GUIDE: *Study Materials, Sample Questions, Mock Exam, Building LEED Certification (LEED-NC) and Going Green,* Book 1,

LEED Exam Guide series, ArchiteG.com (Published September 23, 2008).

LEED GA EXAM GUIDE: A Must-Have for the LEED Green Associate Exam: Comprehensive Study Materials, Sample Questions, Mock Exam, Green Building LEED Certification, and Sustainability (LEED v3.0), Book 2, LEED Exam Guide series, ArchiteG.com (Published October 28, 2009)

LEED BD&C EXAM GUIDE: A Must-Have for the LEED AP BD+C Exam: Comprehensive Study Materials, Sample Questions, Mock Exam, Green Building Design and Construction, LEED Certification, and Sustainability (LEED v3.0), Book 3, LEED Exam Guide series, ArchiteG.com (Published December 18, 2009)

LEED ID&C EXAM GUIDE: A Must-Have for the LEED AP ID+C Exam: Comprehensive Study Materials, Sample Questions, Mock Exam, Green Interior Design and Construction, LEED Certification, and Sustainability, Book 4, LEED Exam Guide series, ArchiteG.com (Published March 8, 2010)

LEED O&M EXAM GUIDE: A Must-Have for the LEED AP O+M Exam: Comprehensive Study Materials, Sample Questions, Mock Exam, Green Building Operations and Maintenance, LEED Certification, and Sustainability (LEED v3.0), Book 5, LEED Exam Guide series, ArchiteG.com

LEED HOMES EXAM GUIDE: *A Must-Have for the LEED AP+ Homes Exam: Comprehensive Study Materials, Sample Questions, Mock Exam, Green Building LEED Certification, and Sustainability*, Book 6, LEED Exam Guide series, ArchiteG.com

LEED ND EXAM GUIDE: *A Must-Have for the LEED AP+ Neighborhood Development Exam: Comprehensive Study Materials, Sample Questions, Mock Exam, Green Building LEED Certification, and Sustainability*, Book 7, LEED Exam Guide series, ArchiteG.com

LEED GA MOCK EXAMS: *Questions, Answers, and Explanations: A Must-Have for the LEED Green Associate Exam, Green Building LEED Certification, and Sustainability*, Book 8, LEED Exam Guide series, ArchiteG.com (Published August 6, 2010)

LEED O&M MOCK EXAMS: *Questions, Answers, and Explanations: A Must-Have for the LEED O&M Exam, Green Building LEED Certification, and Sustainability*, Book 9, LEED Exam Guide series, ArchiteG.com (Published October 6, 2010)

How to order these books:

You can order the books listed above at:
http://outskirtspress.com/agent.php?key=11011&page=leedgaexamguide

OR
http://amazon.com

OR
Any other Amazon site, such as http://amazon.ca, http://amazon.co.uk, http://amazon.co.jp, http://amazon.fr, or http://amazon.de

OR
http://bn.com

Following are some detailed descriptions of each text:

LEED Exam Guide series

Comprehensive Study Materials, Sample Questions, Mock Exam, Building LEED Certification, and Going Green

LEED (Leadership in Energy and Environmental Design) is the most important trend in development and is revolutionizing the construction industry. It has gained tremendous momentum and has a profound impact on our environment. From the LEED Exam Guide series, you will learn how to:

1. Pass the LEED Green Associate Exam and various other LEED AP+ exams (each book will help you with a specific LEED exam).

2. Register and certify a building for LEED certification.

3. Understand the intent of each LEED prerequisite and credit.

4. Calculate points for a LEED credit.

5. Identify the responsible party for each prerequisite and credit.
6. Earn extra credits (exemplary performance) for LEED.

7. Implement the local codes and building standards for prerequisites and credits.

8. Receive points for categories not yet clearly defined by the USGBC.

There is currently NO official GBCI book on any of the LEED exams, and most of the existing books on LEED and LEED AP+ are too expensive and too complicated to be practical or helpful. The pocket guides in the LEED Exam Guide series fill in the blanks, demystify LEED, and uncover the tips, codes, and jargon for LEED, as well as the true meaning of "going green." They will set up a solid foundation and fundamental framework of LEED for you. Each book in the LEED Exam Guide series covers every aspect of one or more specific LEED rating system in plain and concise language, and makes this information understandable to anyone.

These pocket guides are small and easy to carry to read when time permits. They are indispensable books for everyone: administrators; developers; contractors; architects; landscape architects; civil, mechanical, electrical, and plumbing engineers; interns; drafters; designers; and other design professionals.

Why is the LEED Exam Guide series needed?

A number of books are available that you can use to prepare for the LEED exams. Consider the following:

1. USGBC reference guides. You need to select the correct version of the reference guide for your exam.

The USGBC reference guides are comprehensive, but they give too much information. For example, *The LEED 2009 Reference Guide for Green Building Design and Construction (BD&C)* has approximately 700 oversized pages. Many of the calculations in the books are too detailed for the exam. The books are also expensive (approximately $200 each, so most people may not buy them for their personal use, but instead, will seek to share an office copy).

Reading a reference guide from cover to cover is good if you have the time. The problem is that very few people actually have the time to read the whole reference guide. Even if you do read the whole guide, you may not remember the important issues required to pass the LEED exam. You need to reread the material several times before you can remember much of it.

Reading a reference guide from cover to cover without a guidebook is a difficult and inefficient way of preparing for the LEED exams, because you do NOT know what USGBC and GBCI are looking for in the exam.

2. The USGBC workshops and related handouts are concise, but they do not cover extra credits (exemplary performance). The workshops are expensive, costing approximately $450 each.

3. Various books published by third parties are available on Amazon. However, most of them are not very helpful.

There are many books on LEED, but not all are useful.

Each book in the LEED Exam Guide series will fill in the blanks and become a valuable, reliable source.

a. They will give you more information for your money. Each of the books in the LEED Exam Guide series provides more information than the related USGBC workshops.

b. They are exam-oriented and more effective than the USGBC reference guides.

c. They are better than most, if not all, of the other third-party books. They give you comprehensive study materials, sample questions and answers, mock exams and answers, and critical information on building LEED certification and going green. Other third-party books only provide a fraction of this information.

d. They are comprehensive yet concise, small, and easy to carry around. You can read them whenever you have a few spare minutes.

e. They are great timesavers. I have highlighted the important information that you need to understand and MEMORIZE. I also make some acronyms and short sentences to help you easily remember the credit names.

You should devote about 1 to 2 weeks of full-time study to pass each of the LEED exams. I have met people who have spent only 40 hours of study time and passed the exams.

You can find sample texts and other information about the LEED Exam Guide series listed under the Amazon customer discussion section for each available book.

What others are saying about *LEED GA Exam Guide* (Book 2, LEED Exam Guide series):

"Finally! A comprehensive study tool for LEED GA Prep!

"I took the 1-day Green LEED GA course and walked away with a power point binder printed in very small print—which was missing MUCH of the required information (although I didn't know it at the time). I studied my little heart out and took the test, only to fail it by 1 point. Turns out I did NOT study all the material I needed to in order to pass the test. I found this book, read it, marked it up, retook the test, and passed it with a 95%. Look, we all know the LEED GA exam is new and the resources for study are VERY limited. This one's the VERY best out there right now. I highly recommend it."
—ConsultantVA

"Complete overview for the LEED GA exam

"I studied this book for about 3 days and passed the exam ... if you are truly interested in learning about the LEED system and green building design, this is a great place to start."
—K.A. Evans

"A Wonderful Guide for the LEED GA Exam

"After deciding to take the LEED Green Associate exam, I started to look for the best possible study materials and resources. From what I thought would be a relatively easy task, it turned into a tedious endeavor. I realized that there are vast amounts of third-party guides and handbooks. Since the official sites offer little to no help, it became clear to me that my best chance to succeed and pass this exam would be to find the most comprehensive study guide that would not only teach me the topics, but would also give me a great background and understanding of what LEED actually is. Once I stumbled upon Mr. Chen's book, all my needs were answered. This is a great study guide that will give the reader the most complete view of the LEED exam and all that it entails.

"The book is written in an easy-to-understand language and brings up great examples, tying the material to the real world. The information is presented in a coherent and logical way, which optimizes the learning process and does not go into details that will not be needed for the LEED Green Associate Exam, as many other guides do. This book stays dead on topic and keeps the reader interested in the material.

"I highly recommend this book to anyone that is considering the LEED Green Associate Exam. I learned a great deal from this guide, and I am feeling very confident about my chances for passing my upcoming exam."
—Pavel Geystrin

"Easy to read, easy to understand

"I have read through the book once and found it to be the perfect study guide for me. The author does a great job of helping you get into the right frame of mind for the content of the exam. I had started by studying the Green Building Design and Construction reference guide for LEED projects produced by the USGBC. That was the wrong approach, simply too much information with very little retention. At 636 pages in textbook format, it would have been a daunting task to get through it. Gang Chen breaks down the points, helping to minimize the amount of information but maximizing the content I was able to absorb. I plan on going through the book a few more times, and I now believe I have the right information to pass the LEED Green Associate Exam."
—**Brian Hochstein**

"All in one—LEED GA prep material

"Since the LEED Green Associate exam is a newer addition by USGBC, there is not much information regarding study material for this exam. When I started looking around for material, I got really confused about what material I should buy. This LEED GA guide by Gang Chen is an answer to all my worries! It is a very precise book with lots of information, like how to approach the exam, what to study and what to skip, links to online material, and tips and tricks for passing the exam. It is like the 'one stop shop' for the LEED Green Associate Ex-

am. I think this book can also be a good reference guide for green building professionals. A must-have!"
—**SwatiD**

"An ESSENTIAL LEED GA Exam Reference Guide

"This book is an invaluable tool in preparation for the LEED Green Associate (GA) Exam. As a practicing professional in the consulting realm, I found this book to be all-inclusive of the preparatory material needed for sitting the exam. The information provides clarity to the fundamental and advanced concepts of what LEED aims to achieve. A tremendous benefit is the connectivity of the concepts with real-world applications.

"The author, Gang Chen, provides a vast amount of knowledge in a very clear, concise, and logical media. For those that have not picked up a textbook in a while, it is very manageable to extract the needed information from this book. If you are taking the exam, do yourself a favor and purchase a copy of this great guide. Applicable fields: Civil Engineering, Architectural Design, MEP, and General Land Development."
—**Edwin L. Tamang**

Architectural Practice Simplified
A Survival Guide and Checklists for Building Construction and Site Improvements, as well as Tips on Architecture, Building Design, Construction, and Project Management

Learn the Tips, Become One of Those Who Know Architectural Practice, and Thrive in the Construction Industry!

For architectural practice, building design, and the construction industry, there are two kinds of people: those who know, and those who don't. The tips about building design, construction, and project management have been closely guarded by those who know—until now.

Most of the existing books on architectural practice are too expensive, too complicated, and too long to be practical or helpful. This book simplifies the process to make it easier to understand and uncovers the secrets of building design, as well as construction and project management. It sets up a solid foundation and fundamental framework for this field. It covers every aspect of architectural practice in plain and concise language that makes the information accessible to all people. Through practical case studies, the text demonstrates the efficient and proper ways to handle various issues and problems that arise in architectural practice, building design, and the construction industry.

The book is for ordinary people, aspiring young architects, as well as seasoned professionals in the construction industry. For ordinary people, it uncovers the tips of building construction; for aspiring architects, it works as a construction industry survival guide and a guidebook to shorten the process of mastering architectural practice and climbing up the professional ladder. For seasoned architects, it has many checklists to refresh the memory. It is an indispensable reference book for ordinary people, architectural students, interns, drafters, designers, seasoned architects, construction administrators, superintendents, construction managers, contractors, and developers.

You will learn:
1. How to develop your business and work with your client.
2. The entire process of building design and construction, including programming, entitlement, schematic design, design development, construction documents, bidding, and construction administration.
3. How to coordinate with government agencies, such as a county's health department or a city's planning, building, fire, or public works department.
4. How to coordinate with your consultants, including soils, civil, structural, electrical,

mechanical, plumbing engineers, landscape architects, etc.
5. How to create and use your own checklists to provide quality control of your construction documents.
6. How to use various logs (i.e., RFI log, submittal log, field visit log, etc.) and lists (contact list, document control list, distribution list, etc.) to organize and simplify your work.
7. How to respond to RFI issues, CCDs, and review change orders, submittals, etc.
8. How to make your architectural practice a profitable and successful business.

Planting Design Illustrated
A Must-Have for Landscape Architecture
A Holistic Garden Design Guide with
Architectural and Horticultural Insight,
and Ideas from Famous Gardens
in Major Civilizations

One of the most significant books on landscaping!

This is one of the most comprehensive books on planting design. It fills in the blanks of the field and introduces poetry, painting, and symbolism into planting design. It covers in detail the two major systems of planting design: formal planting design and naturalistic planting design. It has numerous line drawings and photos to illustrate the planting design concepts and principles. Through in-depth discussions of historical precedents and practical case studies, it uncovers the fundamental design principles and concepts, as well as the underpinning philosophy for planting design. It is an indispensable reference book for landscape architecture students, designers, architects, urban planners, and ordinary garden lovers.

What Others Are Saying About *Planting Design Illustrated* ...

"I found this book to be absolutely fascinating. You will need to concentrate while reading it, but the effort will be well worth your time."

—Bobbie Schwartz, former president of APLD (Association of Professional Landscape Designers) and author of *The Design Puzzle: Putting the Pieces Together*.

"This is a book that you have to read, and it is more than well worth your time. Gang Chen takes you well beyond what you will learn in other books about basic principles like color, texture, and mass."

—Jane Berger, editor & publisher of gardendesignonline

"As a longtime consumer of gardening books, I am impressed with Gang Chen's inclusion of new information on planting design theory for Chinese and Japanese gardens. Many gardening books discuss the beauty of Japanese gardens, and a few discuss the unique charms of Chinese gardens, but this one explains how Japanese and Chinese history, as well as geography and artistic traditions, bear on the development of each country's style. The material on traditional Western garden planting is thorough and inspiring, too. *Planting Design Illustrated* definitely rewards repeated reading and study. Any garden designer will read it with profit."

—Jan Whitner, editor of the *Washington Park Arboretum Bulletin*

"Enhanced with an annotated bibliography and informative appendices, *Planting Design Illustrated* offers an especially "reader friendly" and practical guide that makes it a very strongly recommended addition to personal, professional, academic, and community library gardening & landscaping reference collection and supplemental reading list."

—Midwest Book Review

"Where to start? *Planting Design Illustrated* is, above all, fascinating and refreshing! Not something the lay reader encounters every day, the book presents an unlikely topic in an easily digestible, easy-to-follow way. It is superbly organized with a comprehensive table of contents, bibliography, and appendices. The writing, though expertly informative, maintains its accessibility throughout and is a joy to read. The detailed and beautiful illustrations expanding on the concepts presented were my favorite portion. One of the finest books I've encountered in this contest in the past 5 years."

—Writer's Digest 16th Annual International Self-Published Book Awards Judge's Commentary

"The work in my view has incredible application to planting design generally and a system approach to what is a very difficult subject to teach, at least in my experience. Also featured is a very beautiful philosophy of garden design principles bordering poetry. It's my strong conviction that this work needs to see the light of day by being published for the use of professionals, students & garden enthusiasts."

—Donald C. Brinkerhoff, FASLA, chairman and CEO of Lifescapes International, Inc.

Index

40/60 rule for LEED, 57
Albedo, 23, 26, 37, 39, 50, 52, 63, 65, 85
American Council for an Energy Efficient Economy (ACEEE), 55, 56
ammonia (NH3), 44
APPA, 83
BAS, 81, 89, 98
Basic Services, 63, 64
blackwater, 23, 46, 51, 67, 71
CFC, 22, 28, 29, 39, 43, 44, 50, 54, 55, 65, 67, 69, 70, 122
CIBSE, 81, 95, 100
CIRs, 36, 45, 62, 71
Cradle-to-cradle, 39, 65
Energy Policy Act (EPAct), 24, 51
FAR, 23, 34, 50, 61
FTE, 139
graywater, 23, 29, 39, 46, 50, 55, 64, 65, 71

Green-e, 25, 28, 40, 52, 54, 76, 80
GWP, 37, 43, 44, 62, 67, 69, 70, 122
Halon, 29, 39, 41, 55, 56, 65, 67
I-BEAM, 84, 96
LEED Rating System Selection Policy, 57, 143
Legionella pneumophila, 87, 93
Level 1 walk-through analysis, 76
Level II Energy Audit, 102
Life cycle analysis, 39, 65
Mnemonics, 58
ODP, 30, 37, 42, 43, 44, 63, 67, 69, 70, 122
Open spaces, 27, 54
process energy, 21, 46, 48, 72
RECs, 40, 66, 85, 90
Regional Priority, 25, 52, 100, 118, 131

regulated (non-process) energy, 21, 49, 72
ROI, 33, 59
Setpoints, 90
SRI, 26, 30, 37, 39, 52, 63, 65, 85, 103
stormwater, 22, 29, 30, 31, 37, 39, 50, 56, 63, 84, 94, 101, 106, 109, 115
TRACI, 123, 124
Zero Emission Vehicles (ZEV), 28, 55